D1645167

THE PARADOX OF SCOTTISH CULTURE

THE WHIDDEN LECTURES

Series I (1956)
The Anatomy of South African Misery
C. W. DE KIEWIET
President, The University of Rochester

Series II (1957)
The Evolution of India
VIJAYA LAKSHMI PANDIT
High Commissioner for India to the United Kingdom

Series III (1958)
Colonial Élites: Rome, Spain and the Americas
SIR RONALD SYME
Camden Professor of Ancient History, University of Oxford

Series IV (1959)
The Hollow Universe
CHARLES DE KONINCK
Professor of the Philosophy of Nature, Laval University

Series V (1960)
Three Aspects of Stuart England
SIR GEORGE CLARK
Provost of Oriel College, Oxford, 1947–57

Series VI (1961) (unpublished)
New Horizons in Biblical Research
W. F. ALBRIGHT
The Oriental Seminary, Johns Hopkins University, Baltimore, Maryland

Series VII (1962)
The Flying Trapeze: Three Crises for Physicists
J. R. OPPENHEIMER
Director of the Institute for Advanced Study, Princeton

Series VIII (1963)
Models and Mystery
IAN T. RAMSEY
Nolloth Professor of the Philosophy of the Christian Religion, University of Oxford

Series IX (1964)
The Paradox of Scottish Culture: The Eighteenth-Century Experience
DAVID DAICHES
Professor of English, University of Sussex

THE WHIDDEN LECTURES FOR 1964

The Paradox of Scottish Culture:
The Eighteenth-Century Experience

DAVID DAICHES

*Professor of English and Dean of the School of English and American
Studies in the University of Sussex*

LONDON
OXFORD UNIVERSITY PRESS
NEW YORK   TORONTO
1964

Oxford University Press, Amen House, London E.C.4.

GLASGOW NEW YORK TORONTO MELBOURNE WELLINGTON
BOMBAY CALCUTTA MADRAS KARACHI LAHORE DACCA
CAPE TOWN SALISBURY NAIROBI IBADAN ACCRA
KUALA LUMPUR HONG KONG

© Oxford University Press 1964

*Printed in Great Britain by
The Alden Press, Oxford*

Foreword

The Whidden Lectures were established in 1954 by E. C. Fox, B.A., LL.D., of Toronto, the senior member of the Board of Governors, to honour the memory of a former Chancellor of McMaster University.

The Reverend Dr. Howard P. Whidden, D.D., LL.D., D.C.L., F.R.S.C., was a man of striking appearance, unusual dignity, deep Christian conviction and ready tolerance. Born in 1871 in Antigonish, Nova Scotia, where his family had settled in 1761 after three-quarters of a century's residence in New England, he attended universities in both Canada (Acadia and McMaster) and the United States (Chicago), and also served as a minister of Baptist churches in both countries (in Ontario, Manitoba and Ohio). From 1913 to 1923 he was President of Brandon College, Manitoba, then an affiliate of McMaster University, and for part of that period (1917–21) he represented Brandon as a Member of Parliament in the Canadian House of Commons at Ottawa. He was appointed administrative head (Chancellor) of McMaster University in 1923 and in 1930 became, in a manner of speaking, its second founder when he directed its transfer from Toronto, where it had been established since 1887, to Hamilton. His broad educational outlook and effective leadership resulted in the University's burgeoning greatly in its new location, and Dr. Whidden was able to retire in 1941 with the comforting conviction that he had built both wisely and well. He died in Toronto in 1952.

The Whidden Lectures of 1964 were delivered by Dr. David Daiches, M.A., D.PHIL., PH.D., F.R.S.L., Dean of the School of English and American Studies at the University of Sussex in England and sometime Fellow of Balliol College, Oxford, and Jesus College, Cambridge. Dr. Daiches elected to speak on the history and culture of Scotland, and more particularly his native Edinburgh, in the eighteenth century. The choice of subject would have gladdened the heart of Dr. Whidden, who was himself of Scottish ancestry, and it was singularly appropriate in a city with as many Scottish associations and traditions as Hamilton, Ontario. The learning and familiarity, the grace and wit, with which Dr. Daiches delighted his large audiences, were such as all readers of the books of one of the greatest of literary critics had come to expect: they made the Whidden Lectures of 1964 an exciting and unforgettable experience.

January 1964   E. T. SALMON
                            Principal of University College
                            McMaster University

Contents

I. The Cultural Consequences of the Union

On Tuesday, 25 March 1707 the last session of Scotland's last Parliament met at Parliament House, Edinburgh, a seventeenth-century building which is now the entrance hall of the Court of Session where advocates perambulate with or without their clients. The High Commissioner, representing Queen Anne, was the second Duke of Queensberry; he had served his mistress with skill, energy, and pertinacity, and it was he who successfully piloted the Treaty of Union between England and Scotland through the Scottish Parliament. Before Lord Seafield, Scotland's last Lord Chancellor, adjourned the Parliament, the Duke of Queensberry made the following speech, as recorded in the official minutes of the proceedings:

My Lords and Gentlemen,
    The Publick Business of this Session being now over it is full time to put an end to it.
    I am perswaded that we and our Posterity will reap the benefit of the Union of the two Kingdoms, and I doubt not, that as this Parliament has had the Honour to conclude it, you will in your several Stations recommend to the People of this Nation, a grateful Sense of Her Majesties Goodness and great Care for the Welfare of Her Subjects, in bringing this important Affair to Perfection, and that you will promote an universal Desire in this Kingdom to

become one in Hearts and Affections, as we are inseparably joyn'd in Interest with our Neighbour Nation.[1]

The universal desire to become one with England spoken of by Queensberry was something of a fiction. Public opinion in Scotland was not in fact eager for the union, as numerous protests addressed to Parliament from different parts of the country made clear. The Kirk also made a formal protest, even though 'the Government of the Church, as by Law Established in *Scotland*'—to quote the assurance given by Queen Anne herself[2]—was secured in the treaty. Severe anti-union riots broke out in both Edinburgh and Glasgow, despite the fact that the latter city, made free by the treaty of union to trade with English colonial markets in the New World, was to build a rapid commercial prosperity on this freedom. The union was nevertheless made inevitable by the consequences of the Union of the Crowns in 1603. When a Scottish king moved south to London to become king of England as well as of Scotland, it was natural that he should subordinate the interests of the smaller and poorer country to those of the richer and larger. The stronger the influence of Parliament in England, the more difficult it was for the king to govern with two separate and quite differently based Parliaments—the English and the Scottish—simultaneously. The 'Glorious Revolution' of 1688 established the monarchy as a limited one. The matter has been well summed up by Douglas Nobbs: 'Limited monarchy in conjunction with the Union of Crowns gave to the king's English ministers the indirect rule of Scotland, and the means to sacrifice Scottish

[1] *Minutes of the Proceedings in Parliament*, Number 89 (Edinburgh, Printed by the Heirs and Successors of Andrew Anderson, 1707).

[2] *Her Majestie's Most Gracious Letter to the Parliament of Scotland* (Edinburgh, Printed by the Heirs and Successors of Andrew Anderson, 1706).

interests to English prosperity.'[3] Scottish discontent at being managed from London by English ministers suggested in some quarters that a reversion to a separate Scottish king would guarantee proper attention to Scottish interests. Though this was recognized by most thoughtful people as an extreme and indeed as an anachronistic measure, and though nobody on either side of the Border wished a renewal of the ancient and traditional warfare between England and Scotland, the threat by the Scottish Parliament to determine the succession to the Scottish throne independently of the way in which it was determined in England forced English politicians to see an 'incorporating union' between England and Scotland as the only way to close the Scottish back door—as it was often put—and to prevent Scotland becoming again an independent kingdom that could ally herself with England's enemies or give aid and comfort to claimants to the English throne who had been repudiated by the English government.

The Scots, humiliated, outraged, and impoverished by the total failure of the Darien scheme, their first ambitious attempt to found a colony in the New World for trading purposes, and attributing that failure to the hostility and deliberate obstruction of English trading interests, bitterly resented their exclusion from English colonial markets. This helped to increase Scottish pride and touchiness. To the English, the Scots were poor, proud, and politically dangerous; to the Scots, the English were rich, arrogant, and obstructive. Yet a deal could be done—indeed, the nature of the mutual hostility between the two countries determined the sort of deal that could be carried through. If Scotland would drop her attempts to take an independent line on the succession question, England, by means of an incorporating union

[3] *England and Scotland, 1560–1707*, by Douglas Nobbs (London, 1952).

between the two countries, would throw open English—
they would now be British—colonial markets to the Scots and
make possible (so the argument ran) vast economic improvements in Scotland. England would have her back door
permanently shut and Scotland could share in England's
economic opportunities. Scotland, of course, would lose her
independence as a nation, for this was to be an incorporating
and not a federal union, in spite of the preference of a considerable number of those Scotsmen who supported union at
all for the latter variety. A federal union was unacceptable to
the English government: they felt safer with total incorpora-
tion. Scotland was to keep her Church and her legal system,
but her Parliament was to go. Instead, Scotland would send
forty-five members to the House of Commons at Westminster
(one more than were sent by the sparsely populated English
county of Cornwall) and sixteen Scottish peers, elected by the
total Scottish peerage from among themselves, to the House
of Lords.

Whether the undoubted improvement in the economic
state of Scotland in the eighteenth century was the direct
result of the Union has been debated. 'The Union did not,
within a generation, bring to Scotland the economic advantages which had been so confidently predicted. It is true that
fifty years after the Union an era of prosperity set in, which
transformed the industrial and commercial life of the country.
But although this prosperity has been generally, and even
enthusiastically, ascribed to the Union, it is doubtful how
far that attribution is correct.'[4] So speaks the modern bio-
grapher of the bitterest opponent of an incorporating union to
sit in the Scottish Parliament that voted it, and against this

[4] *Andrew Fletcher of Saltoun*, by W. C. Mackenzie (Edinburgh, 1935),
p. 285.

4

we may set the words of Scott's Bailie Nicol Jarvie: 'Whisht, sir!—whisht!' he cried to Andrew Fairservice when the latter complained of the Union. 'It's ill-scraped tongues like yours that make mischief between neighbourhoods and nations. There's naething sae gude on this side o' time but it might have been better, and that may be said o' the Union. Nane were keener against it than the Glasgow folk, wi' their rabblings and their risings, and their mobs, as they ca' them nowadays. But it's an ill wind that blaws naebody gude—let ilka ane roose the ford as they find it.—I say, let Glasgow flourish! whilk is judiciously and elegantly putten round the town's arms by way of by word. Now, since St. Mungo catched herrings in the Clyde, what was ever like to gar us flourish like the sugar and tobacco trade? Will anybody tell me that, and grumble at a treaty that opened us a road west-awa' yonder?'

At any rate, the opening of the eighteenth century was a time of bitter economic hardship for Scotland. The 'seven ill years' that began in 1696, brought a succession of failed harvests and resulting famine. Year after year cold, wet summers and freezing autumns wrought havoc with the country's agriculture. In 1698 Fletcher of Saltoun, moved by 'the condition of so many thousands of our people who are, at this day, dying for want of bread',[5] produced a plan for the relief of poverty and unemployment and the reduction of the vast number of beggars, which he put at two hundred thousand.[6] But no plans for compulsory labour, such as that propounded by Fletcher, or indeed no plans of any kind, could change Scottish conditions without substantial economic

[5] *The Second Discourse Concerning the Affairs of Scotland*, in *Political Works of Andrew Fletcher, Esq., of Saltoun* (Glasgow, 1749), p. 84.
[6] ibid., p. 100.

growth. The famine of 1696–1703 exposed the precariousness and the vulnerability of the Scottish economy as well as
the primitiveness of Scottish agriculture. In the early part of
the eighteenth century arable land throughout the country
was still cultivated on the primitive and wasteful infield and
outfield system, and tenants owned scattered strips or 'rigs' of
land, generally crooked S-shaped ridges flanked by banks of
weeds.[7] The old wooden plough, which required a team
of eight to twelve oxen to draw it, was still in wide use, being
indeed well suited for really rough land; harrows were also
wooden and pulled by hand; corn was threshed with the flail
and ground in mills to which tenants were bound to take their
corn and pay lavishly for having it ground and even for not
having it ground. Shortage of winter cattle-feed led to a
high mortality of cattle and sheep during the winter.[8] As for
the social organization of the countryside, it was essentially
a landlord-and-tenant system, with the landlords often
having legal claims on their tenants for services as well as for
produce; until the abolition of heritable jurisdictions in
1747 land ownership in Scotland could also mean,
especially in the Highlands, the power to try, judge, and
punish a tenant.

Agricultural improvement went on sporadically and un-
evenly, but very definitely, throughout the century, under the
influence of the example of Holland, where so many budding
lawyers went from Scotland to study Roman Law, on which
much Scots law was based, and of England, where visiting
Scottish landowners picked up not only new agricultural
methods but also English farmers to advise and help. To
improve methods of farming on one's estate, to import seeds,

[7] *An Economic History of Scotland in the Eighteenth Century*, by Henry Hamilton
(Oxford, 1963), chapter II.   [8] ibid.

6

to plant trees—these became favourite preoccupations of the more enlightened Scottish gentry in the eighteenth century and sometimes went along with an interest in literature and the arts. It would be hard not to credit the Union with some of this activity: the Union certainly facilitated movement between Scotland and England.

In these improvements the landowners rarely had the support of their tenants, who looked with suspicion on all new-fangled and foreign methods. Even as late as 1811 the writer of the *Agricultural Report* on Ayrshire complained that 'an extensive acquaintance with the mysterious, abstruse and disputed points of systematic divinity, was the species of knowledge they generally sought after, and to which the greatest fame was attached'.[9] This reference to religious interests on the part of tenant farmers is a symptom of the disruptive part that religion often played in eighteenth-century Scotland, as we shall see. Religion played a unifying part too, helping to focus certain kinds of Scottish national feeling that were left with few institutional outlets after the Union. The church and the law were the two national institutions left to Scotland after 1707. The law was the prerogative of an educated professional class, a small but influential minority in the country, who were largely responsible for the re-definition of polite culture in eighteenth-century Scotland. The church had more widespread and in some sense more democratic influence, and the numerous splits and secessions from the established Church of Scotland between Erskine's secession of 1734 and the Disruption of 1843 is an indication of how ecclesiastical replaced political controversy and responded to various currents of national feeling.

Agricultural improvement was associated with gentility,

9 ibid., p. 73.

even with theological laxness or at least moderatism; sometimes also with benevolence. Model villages as well as well-
laid-out gardens were among the works of the improvers.
Yet one senses a lack of organic relation to rural society as a
whole in much of this activity, rather parallel to the position
of the Edinburgh *literati* with reference to the deeper cultural
traditions of Scotland. The tone is very nicely indicated by
Ramsay of Ochtertyre, writing about Lord Kames—who
was both an agricultural improver and one of the *literati*.

About 1747 or 1748, his lordship made his first essays in husbandry at Kames. It is needless to enquire whether it was a gaining
adventure. It was to him for a number of years a source of much
entertainment; for like Cato the Censor, he might have said, '*Agrico-
larum voluptatibus incredibiliter delector*'. Indeed farming was one
of the sciences in which he wished to be thought as learned as in
jurisprudence or ethics. He deserves great praise for the part which
he had in introducing English husbandry into Scotland. And for a
number of years he strained every nerve to inspire all his friends and
neighbours with a passion for it as ardent as his own ... Mean-
while he enriched his domains and embellished his place, grudging
no expense or exertion. And he gave a good example to his tenants
and neighbours. Though little partial in those days to gentlemen
farmers, they were indebted to him for great improvements in
ploughing, and for certain implements of husbandry, which he
either bribed or forced them to use. The Bridge of Drip, and the
colony which he planted in the moss, remain honourable monuments
of his enterprise and perseverance—the latter being a small addition
to the sum total of human happiness. To borrow an expression
from one of his own inscriptions, it was engrafting benevolence on
self-love, which is the way to have excellent and valuable fruit.[10]

Agricultural improvement in eighteenth-century Scotland
was thus largely the work of benevolent or patronizing or

[10] *Scotland and Scotsmen in the Eighteenth Century*. From the MSS. of John
Ramsay, Esq. of Ochtertyre, edited by Alexander Allardyce (Edinburgh, 1888),
vol. i, pp. 207–8.

ambitious landowners, a class whose relation to Scottish national culture as a whole remained, as we shall see, curiously ambiguous. Even improvement in commerce and industry was, in its earlier stages at least, the work of doctrinaire improvers rather than of spontaneous economic development. The Board of Trustees for Improving Fisheries and Manufactures in Scotland, set up by the government in 1727, devoted itself energetically to the development of the Scottish linen industry and its deliberate encouragement of improved standards of weaving and of new techniques of manufacture were important factors in the spectacular growth of the industry throughout the century. The Convention of Royal Burghs also interested itself in promoting trade and manufactures, and made special efforts to help both the linen industry and herring fishing. The Forfeited Estates Commissioners, appointed in 1752 to manage the estates forfeited by Jacobite rebels after the rebellion of 1745, also exerted themselves to assist Scottish manufactures, especially in the Highlands: in 1753 Parliament granted from the proceeds of these estates an annual sum of £3,000 for nine years to help the linen industry in the Highlands.[11] And in 1754 there was founded the Edinburgh Society for Encouraging Arts, Sciences, Manufactures, and Agriculture, which not only discussed Scotland's economic problems but also offered prizes for conspicuous agricultural and industrial achievement. Indeed, wherever one looks in the economic history of Scotland in the eighteenth century one is struck by the number of bodies, both public and private, whose function was to encourage, improve, and reward Scottish economic development.

This, of course, is not even the merest sketch of Scotland's economic development in the eighteenth century, but I have

[11] Hamilton, op. cit., p. 146.

picked out these few facts in order to suggest part of an answer to the question with which I started. 'Did Scotland benefit from the Union?' The answer is: Yes, economically at least, in certain ways, but even here that benefit was achieved in some significant areas by imposition from above, and this fact is itself symbolic of some of the paradoxes of Scotland's nationhood since 1707. The stubborn tenant farmers who resisted Fletcher of Saltoun's winnowing machine (for many years the only such machine in Scotland) on the grounds that it interfered with the will of God are typical of many such situations in eighteenth-century Scotland. Just as there steadily developed a cleavage between genteel culture and popular culture, which adversely affected both, so there was something ambiguous about even economic development. Lord Kames imposing agricultural improvements on reluctant farmers and Robert Burns resisting the demands of the Edinburgh *literati* that he should write a more conventional kind of poetry and become a member of the literary Establishment, can be compared with the farmers who resisted new techniques on theological grounds. Their attitude was far from Luddite; it was, in an odd way, national. It is related to the way in which, later in the century, genuine Gaelic literature still being produced in Scotland was neglected in favour of high-minded inquiries into the nature of primitive poetry such as Gaelic poetry was supposed to be and defences of Macpherson's spurious *Ossian*. This relationship will, I hope, emerge later. It is bound up with a split, or a series of splits, in the whole national ethos of Scotland, of which the Union was one significant cause. This is not to say that the Union should not have taken place; it was perhaps inevitable; and it was bound up with other causes which go much further back into Scottish history.

The Union in the long run did produce forces which worked consciously for the improvement of agriculture and industry in Scotland, but those forces were bound up with elements that seemed at the same time to militate against a national culture or even at times (as in the case of the Highland clearances) against national prosperity. The paradox was not, however, a new one: it represented something in which Scottish life and Scottish culture had already been involved for some time in 1707. If the Union of the Crowns in 1603 meant that a king of both England and Scotland inevitably sacrificed the interests of his smaller to those of his larger country, and if the growth of English parliamentary influence on the Crown increased this tendency, this did not mean that the incorporating union of 1707 in any way diminished it. English influence, both political and cultural, inevitably increased. The departure of James VI for England in 1603 had meant the abrupt cessation of the court patronage of the arts in Scotland and the physical departure of poets and musicians as well as the rapidly increasing influence of the English language and English literature on the language and literature of Scotland. But even before this the Reformation had broken across the traditional cultural boundaries and interests of Scotland, bringing about new ties with the 'auld enemy' England, now a Protestant country, and weakening ties with Scotland's old ally, France. The use of a Protestant English translation of the Bible in Scotland is only one symptom of this. As for the political and religious controversies of the seventeenth century, they produced attitudes which cut across linguistic and even national lines with consequences that can be very confusing for the cultural historian.

The literary sophistication of late medieval Scottish literature, as seen in the poetry of Henryson and Dunbar and the other Scottish 'makars', reflected an artistic scrupulousness which is still seen in the last two decades of the sixteenth century at the Court of James VI where there was a centre of both literary and musical activity. This sophistication did not survive the permanent departure of the Court in 1603 except in isolated pockets, notably in the north-east. And although echoes of the lost court poetry are to be found in various mutated and sometimes popularized forms throughout the seventeenth century and indeed into the eighteenth, on the whole it is true to say that ever since 1603 Scottish poetry and Scottish music were drawing more and more on a popular and less and less on a courtly or sophisticated tradition. In music, the native air (i.e. the airs of *dance songs*) steadily superseded court song and polyphonic music, while in poetry those poets who did not emigrate to England and write in English in an English tradition either wrote in Scotland in English for an English audience or turned to a regional vernacular poetry in a spirit of sociological condescension, patriotic feeling, or antiquarian revival.

1707 provided a political solution to what for the English had become an otherwise insoluble problem; to the Scots it represented inevitably an ultimate political defeat and, as Scotland's last Lord Chancellor put it, whether in sorrow or in irony, 'the end of an auld sang'. Scottish pride was hurt, and one reaction made itself felt immediately—the turning to the Scottish literary past in order to record and circulate some of the achievements of a time when Scotland had a genuine literature of its own. W. B. Yeats wrote in 1890: 'We are preparing, likely enough, for a new Irish literary movement ... that will show itself in the first lull in politics.' That lull came—or seemed to Yeats to have come—with the death of Parnell in October 1891, and Yeats bestirred himself to provide a literary equivalent for the lost political impetus. Something very similar seems to have happened in Scotland when the incorporating union was being argued in the Scottish Parliament. In 1706, the crucial year of debate about the Union in Scotland, James Watson brought out the first of his three volumes entitled *A Choice Collection of Comic and Serious Scots Poems both Ancient and Modern.* This collection, of which the second and third volumes appeared in 1709 and 1711, described by its editor as being 'the first of its Nature which has been publish'd in our own Native *Scots* Dialect', was an attempt to make contact with Scotland's literary past. The motives that prompted it were patriotic, and it is relevant to consider just who James Watson was.

Watson was an Edinburgh printer of skill and enterprise who was involved throughout much of his turbulent life in a fight against the claims of a printing monopoly maintained by the widow of Andrew Anderson, the late King's Printer.[12] In her struggle to maintain her monopoly against Watson, Mrs. Anderson charged that he had been bred a Papist and printed Popish and Jacobitical books, and it is true at least that (as well as referring to Charles I as the 'Royal Martyr') he was an ardent Scottish patriot who had got into trouble in 1700 for printing a pamphlet, entitled *People of Scotland's Groans and Lamentable Complaints Pour'd out before the High Court of Parliament*, a bitter and eloquent protest against the treatment of Scotland in the matter of the Darien disaster. This pamphlet was part of a larger work by Hugh Paterson entitled *A Scottish Grievance relating to Darien ... humbly*

[12] Much of the story is told, from Watson's point of view, in his 'Publisher's Preface to the Printers in Scotland', prefixed to his *History of the Art of Printing* (largely translated from the French), Edinburgh, 1713. Watson gives an interesting picture of the state of printing in Scotland in the late seventeenth and early eighteenth centuries.

offered to the consideration of Parliament, also printed by Watson, and both author and printer were jailed for the offence, though shortly afterwards delivered from prison by a popular rising. After that Watson seems to have diverted his Scottish partiotism to more literary channels: in addition to printing Bibles, catechisms, and other religious works agreeable to the Church of Scotland (which suggests that he must have shed any Roman Catholic tendencies he may have had), he published in 1718 *The Famous History of the Renown'd and Valiant Prince, Robert, sirnamed the Bruce, King of Scotland*, by Patrick Gordon, a work in couplet verse which had first appeared at Dort in 1615, and in 1719 he printed the popular imitation ballad 'Hardyknute'. But the three volumes of his *Choice Collection* represent the most important manifestation of his Scottish patriotism.

It is important to establish Watson's motives and to glance at his character and history in order to demonstrate the relation between Scottish national feeling and the interest in making available older Scottish literature which developed out of the Union. That Watson had at one time been a Jacobite is also relevant. The development of Jacobite sentiment into Scottish national feeling was a direct consequence of the debate about the Union that went on in Scotland between 1703 and 1707. Much of the most vocal Scottish national feeling in the 1680s and 1690s had been Protestant and Whig, and the type of Scottish patriot at the turn of the century was that eloquent and bitter opponent of an incorporating union, the anti-Jacobite, anti-monarchist Andrew Fletcher of Saltoun. When the Duke of York (later James VII of Scotland and II of England) was in Scotland in 1680–1, representing his brother Charles II as Lord High Commissioner, his behaviour outraged popular Protestant feeling in

Scotland, so that support for the House of Stuart at this time was far from being identified in the nation at large as a patriotic Scottish national position. It was only after the Stuarts were exiled that they became a romantic lost cause identified by much Scottish popular feeling with the lost glory and independence of the Scottish nation. Even the Massacre of Glencoe and the Darien disaster did not achieve any immediate swing of Scottish national feeling as a whole to the House of Stuart. But the debate about the Union did. We can in fact identify the precise moment when, in the Scottish Parliament, the Cavaliers committed themselves to the side of Scottish independence and Scottish patriotism: it was on 26 May 1703, when the Act of Security, designed to protect Scottish rights with respect to the succession and other matters, was being debated. The Cavaliers voted with the patriots, and because the other elements with whom they voted eventually became, for one reason or another, identified with the Union, the Cavaliers remained in a considerable section of Scottish public opinion as champions of Scottish independence. In other words, the Union was largely responsible for the process by which the House of Stuart, whose devotion to their own English interests in the seventeenth century had so reduced the national position of Scotland, became in the Scottish imagination the symbol of a proud, free, independent Scotland lost in 1707.

This point is worth pausing on, because it explains the continued appeal of a 'sentimental Jacobitism' (in Burns's phrase) among Scots throughout the eighteenth century, even Scots who, like Burns himself, were deeply democratic and anti-monarchist in feeling. I have already quoted Bailie Nicol Jarvie's defence of the Union from Scott's *Rob Roy*. Side by side with that we should put Redgauntlet's explanation of his Jacobite enthusiasm years after the failure of the '45 in Scott's *Redgauntlet*. He associates Jacobitism with Scottish independence and the restoration of the exiled House of Stuart with the war of independence successfully fought against the English by Robert the Bruce in the early fourteenth century.[13] Anachronistic and historically meaningless as the Jacobite movement was, it nevertheless provided—for historical reasons which can be precisely identified—a focus for Scottish national feeling. The very fact that the cause was lost helped to turn Scottish national feeling into something elegiac and literary and is one reason—the other is the unassimilated effects of the industrial revolution on the Scottish imagination—for the incurable nostalgia of much Scottish literature especially in the nineteenth century.

It is, therefore, relevant to note that James Watson, whose *Choice Collection* marked the beginning of the eighteenth-century Scottish literary revival, had Jacobite sympathies and published a verse account of the patriotic exploits of Robert the Bruce. The *Choice Collection* was an attempt to make contact with Scotland's literary past; in his somewhat odd assortment of sixteenth- and seventeenth-century poems Watson saw himself as serving up to his countrymen what was still available of poetry written in an older tradition. Here were seventeenth-century songs of popular revelry—but printed as poems, with no indication that they were songs—side by side with 'The Cherry and the Slae', that strange, complex poem in medieval Rose tradition by James VI's chief court poet, William Montgomerie. Here too were Montgomerie's elaborate and haunting allegorical poem, 'The Solsequium'

---

[13] For a fuller discussion of this point, see my essay on *Redgauntlet* in *From Jane Austen to Joseph Conrad*, edited by Robert C. Rathburn and Martin Steinmann (Minneapolis, 1958), pp. 46–59.

(marigold) and Robert Sempill's deliberately vulgar, rollicking poem, 'The Life and Death of the Piper of Kilbarchan or the Epitaph of Habbie Simson', a seventeenth-century mock elegy written in a very old stanza form which was to provide both a literary genre and a standard verse form (the so-called 'Burns stanza') to eighteenth-century Scottish poetry, notably to Burns. The opening poem of volume one is 'Christ's Kirk on the Green', an influential poem of popular revelry in a traditional Scottish mode attributed to James V: Watson printed the poem in a simplified stanza form and in this form it passed on to Fergusson and Burns. This is followed by 'The Blythsome Wedding', a much later song in the same tradition, a tradition by now vulgarized so that this is more like early-twentieth-century music hall than either true folk song or serious art. The third poem, 'The Banishment of Poverty', by 'J. D. of *Albany*', actually by Francis Sempill, an interesting late-seventeenth-century poem in a mixture of styles, done with considerable vigour and liveliness in first-person narrative, telling of the predicament of an impoverished Tory gentleman who finally sought sanctuary against arrest for debt in the precincts of Holyrood, where he was lucky enough to see the Duke of Albany (the Duke of York, later James VII and II), who banished his poverty with 'one blink of his princely eye'. Poems of compliment in undistinguished English octosyllabic couplets; poems of satire on contemporary fashion sometimes in English, sometimes partly in Scots; 'The Mare of Colintoun', a long humorous poem in racy Scots telling of the mare's sufferings, last will and testament, and death, and thus bringing into the eighteenth century a tradition of mock testament and animal poetry which represents a modification of the medieval beast fable possessing a vitality of its own from which Burns was to profit; William Hamilton's 'Last Dying Words of Bonny Heck, a Famous Greyhound in the Shire of Fife', an early-eighteenth-century poem in the 'Habbie Simson' tradition—this extraordinary mixed bunch precede six poems by Montgomerie, which look very strange beside the late jocular vernacular poetry. Then comes a poem in Dog-Latin or Latin-Scots by Drummond of Hawthornden, written in a clever-schoolboy sort of way, followed by 'Hallow my Fancie', a poem in English with a fine, sprightly movement and showing a lively humorous imagination by an unknown author but containing ten stanzas by Colonel William Cleland, a Covenanting poet who consciously tried to establish a non-courtly serious satiric Scottish poetic tradition.

A mixed bag, indeed! The next two volumes were equally mixed, with a great variety of poems old and new with the texts of the older poems in varying degrees of corruption or anglicization. Translations from Latin, macaronics, courtly poems in English, a poem in the old Scottish flyting tradition, a broadside text of an early version of 'Auld Lang Syne' entitled 'Old Long Syne', eight poems by Montrose (the substantial part of Montrose's poetry), and a variety of epigrams and imitations. What did Watson's anthology add up to? Surprisingly enough, it did represent with some accuracy what was available for reconstructing a Scottish poetic tradition. The tradition of the makars was represented by Montgomerie (Dunbar and Henryson were not made available until later, by Allan Ramsay); the courtly tradition was represented by Drummond and Aytoun; the popular tradition was represented in its older phase by 'Christ's Kirk on the Green' and in its newer by 'Habbie Simson', and other poems represented in different ways characteristic varieties of Scottish humour and Scottish violence as well as the goliardic tradition in its Scottish form and the tradition of macaronic humour that developed out of it.

In making these things available, Watson inevitably changed their nature. For example, his collection gives no indication that 'Habbie Simson', 'The Solsequium', and the lullaby called 'Lady Anne Bothwell's Balow' ever went to music. Indeed, the elaborate stanza forms used by Montgomerie, originally so closely related to the musical setting, finally lose all connexion with music in Watson and begin a new life in Scottish poetry as vehicles for a rhetorical spoken verse. Scottish song, which as we shall see developed a vigorous new life in the eighteenth century, loses contact with its more sophisticated past, and develops later in the century a new and wholly inappropriate sophistication under the all-pervasive Italian musical influence.

I have mentioned the linguistic confusion shown in some of the poems in Watson. This is bound up with the whole problem of the Scots language, a problem which was never solved in the eighteenth century. In the golden age of Scottish poetry, the age of the makars, Scots was a full-blooded literary language, based on the spoken language of the people but enriched by the poets with a great variety of linguistic devices and inventions which had their own peculiarly Scottish relationship to their Latin and other sources. This language, Middle Scots, had originally been identical with the Anglian speech of northern England, and remained closely related to English even though by the fifteenth century it had developed into a mature, complex, and expressive language in its own right. From the late sixteenth century on, this Scottish literary language was increasingly challenged by English. The Reformation, the Union of the Crowns in 1603, the political and religious

19

situation in the seventeenth century, and finally the Union of 1707, all had their effect in helping to make Scottish writers turn to English as their medium even though they continued to speak in Scots. In these circumstances, there steadily ceased to be a Scots literary language, rooted in the spoken language yet continuously reaching out beyond it, capable of expressing the whole thinking and feeling man. Without a literary standard of written Scots to hold the language together, Scots degenerated into a series of regional dialects with no recognized orthography, to be transcribed in patronizing or antiquarian or nostalgic mood as though it were a quaint sort of English.

Scots, that characteristic northern form of English with its own logical pattern of sound changes, its own relation to Anglo-Saxon, and its own techniques of borrowing and of developing new formations, was thus reduced from a language to a vernacular, and its differences from southern English came to be seen even by patriotic Scotsmen as representing corruption. 'Is it not strange', wrote David Hume to Gilbert Elliot of Minto on 2 July 1757, 'that, at a time when we have lost our Princes, our Parliaments, our independent Government, even the presence of our chief Nobility, are unhappy, in our accent & Pronunciation, speak a very corrupt Dialect of the Tongue which we make use of; is it not strange, I say, that, in these Circumstances, we shou'd really be the People most distinguish'd for Literature in Europe?'[14] Here is patriotic Scottish pride going side by side with the belief that the Scots language is 'a very corrupt dialect' of English. In 1787 Professor James Beattie of Aberdeen produced a book entitled *Scotticisms, arranged in Alphabetical Order, designed*

[14] *Letters of David Hume*, edited by J. Y. T. Grieg (Oxford, 1932), vol. i, p. 255.

to correct Improprieties of Speech and Writing. Beattie, a bad philosopher and an indifferent poet, was much concerned to enable Scotsmen to write in southern English with no taint of their native speech. He wanted, he says in his introduction, 'to put young writers and speakers on their guard against some of those Scotch idioms, which, in this country, are liable to be mistaken for English. With respect to broad Scotch words I do not think any caution requisite, as they are easily known, and the necessity of avoiding them is obvious.' In 1761 the Irish actor and lecturer on elocution, Thomas Sheridan (father of the dramatist), lectured in his Irish brogue to entranced members of the Select Society of Edinburgh on the proper pronunciation of English.[15]

These are symptoms of a 'dissociation of sensibility' in Scotland much more marked than that which Mr. T. S. Eliot so memorably diagnosed in the English poetic scene. If you talk and, as it were, feel in Scots and think and write in standard English,[16] then your Scots is likely to be sentimental and self-indulgent and your English is likely to be highly formal and in some degree de-natured. The expository, historical, and philosophical prose of eighteenth-century Scotsmen is often very fine, because these are areas of communication in which the formal discipline of a method of expression acquired at school was helpful. Scottish poetry, when written in English, was often (but not invariably) derivative and stilted, and when written in Scots was always in

[15] As late as 1774 Boswell noted as a matter of some interest that 'a little one-eyed clergyman', whom he met at the house of John Francis Erskine in Alloa 'spoke English'. *Boswell: The Ominous Years*, edited by Charles Ryskamp and F. A. Pottle. London, 1963, p. 21.

[16] Writing of Scotland between 1745 and 1763 Ramsay of Ochtertyre (op. cit., vol. i, p. 310) remarked: 'Nobody now doubted the possibility of a Scotsman writing pure, nay, even elegant, English, whilst he spoke his native dialect a little diversified.'

danger of being self-consciously humorous or low or 'quaint'. Eighteenth-century Scottish literary criticism, which is almost entirely concerned with rhetoric, with the study of formal devices for stirring the emotions, is generally quite incapable of dealing with the more subtle and impressive devices of combining rational and emotional appeal to achieve richness of expression and tends to mistake floridity for eloquence, pathos for tragedy, and sentimental declamation for poetry. The reception of Macpherson's *Ossian* is evidence of this or, to take a more particular case, Henry Mackenzie's review of Burns's Kilmarnock volume in *The Lounger*, which praised some of the weakest and most sentimental of Burns's stanzas as being 'solemn and sublime, with ... rapt and inspired melancholy'.

The philosophers, historians and critics of the second half of the eighteenth-century Edinburgh, the *literati* as they liked to call themselves, were in their way patriotic Scotsmen (witness David Hume's pride in his countrymen's literary achievements) but they felt that the way for Scotsmen to demonstrate their national greatness was to avoid in their writing the language they naturally spoke and write a carefully composed standard English. In this way, they believed, with some logic, they could reach a wider audience. Indeed, they might be thought of as using English as earlier scholars and thinkers had used Latin in order to reach an international public. At the same time, from the very moment when the Union was about to be passed by the Scottish Parliament, a quite different tradition was developing. This tradition, which had already been anticipated by some writers in the late seventeenth century, was concerned with the Scots language, and sought ways in which poetry in Scots could still be written. Such poetry was bound now to be a dialect poetry, as the Scots literary language had virtually disappeared, even though a particular regional dialect could be enriched by older Scottish forms taken from literary sources or by forms deliberately taken from other regions. It was too late to do anything for Scots prose, which was later to find some attenuated prolongation of life in dialogue in Scottish novels, but poetry drawing on the folk tradition rather than on a more complex art tradition, poetry of rustic merriment, of urban low life, of conviviality or abuse or courtship—this was a way of keeping Scots still usable in literature and the way was shown notably by Allan Ramsay.

Ramsay came from Leadhills, Lanarkshire, to Edinburgh about 1700 at the age of sixteen or seventeen and there until his death in 1758 he engaged in a variety of literary and other activities which perfectly symbolize some of the confusions in Scottish culture and Scottish national feeling after the Union. Beginning as a wigmaker and then turning writer and bookseller, Ramsay wanted from an early age to turn himself into a gentleman. He was a co-founder in 1712 of the Easy Club, established by a group of young men 'in order that by a Mutual improvement in Conversation they may become more adapted for fellowship with the politer part of mankind and Learn also from one another's happy observations'.[17] (Burns later founded the Tarbolton Bachelors' Club with the same end in view.) He had his eyes on the Queen Anne wits in London, and tried, not very successfully, to become a Scottish equivalent. At the same time he was a violently patriotic Scot who aimed at both reviving interest in older Scottish literature and in producing Scots poetry of his own. At the Easy Club they read the *Spectator* and, the members of

[17] *Allan Ramsay: A Study of his Life and Works*, by Burns Martin (Cambridge, Mass.), p. 25.

the Club all having pseudonyms, Ramsay adopted that of Isaac Bickerstaff. But at the end of 1713 Ramsay changed his Easy Club pseudonym to Gavin Douglas, thus suggesting that as well as providing encouragement to behave like English gentlemen the Easy Club also provided a background of Scottish national sentiment. The Club also gave Ramsay the opportunity to demonstrate his flair for writing 'occasional' verse. Ramsay was a facile topical versifier with his eye on Pope and Gay and Matthew Prior. But he had had his eye also on Scotland's past and on the present Scots vernacular. In 1718 he brought out, anonymously on broadsides, several editions of 'Christ's Kirk on the Green', with supplementary verses of his own in a Scots partly contemporary and partly antique or fake antique. These added stanzas possess considerable vigour, but they show a self-conscious determination to be one of the boys which distinguishes their tone at once from the mood of genuine folk celebration we find in the original. In the same year Ramsay published a series of Scots poems on Edinburgh low life in which he shows a lively command of the vernacular. In these poems—elegies on Maggy Johnston, John Cowper, and Lucky Wood, all in the mock-elegy tradition of 'Habbie Simson'—Scots could be used without any air of antiquarian reconstruction, for the characters who figured in them were part of the Scots-speaking ordinary life of the city. Ramsay went on to produce other poems in the same vein, but at the same time continued with his more genteel productions. Sometimes his Scottish feeling vented itself in a poem written in stiff heroic couplets in a stilted conventional English, as in 'Tartana: Or, The Plaid', a passionate defence of native Scottish customs where the disparity between form and content is startling. A more successful poetic form developed by Ramsay was the vernacular verse letter, where the informal colloquial style made a spoken Scots wholly appropriate: both Fergusson and Burns were to make admirable use of this tradition.

In the preface to the volume of his poems published in 1721 Ramsay admitted cheerfully that he had 'small Knowledge of dead or foreign Languages' and argued that this was no disadvantage. 'King David, Homer and Virgil, say they [i.e. say the critics to Ramsay] were more ignorant of the Scots and English Tongue, than you are of Hebrew, Greek and Latin: Pursue your own natural Manner, and be an original'. Thus the use of Scots is associated with ignorance of the classics and with cultural parochialism—an attitude which would have horrified Dunbar and Henryson and the other Middle Scots poets, if indeed it would have been comprehensible to them. There is often an exhibitionist quality about Ramsay's use of Scots, as though he was presenting a provincial vernacular for the amusement of the educated. 'The *Scotticisms*, which perhaps may offend some over-nice Ear, give new Life and Grace to the Poetry, and become their Place as well as the *Doric* dialect of *Theocritus*, so much admired by the best Judges'. This sentence from the 1721 preface argues both a certain defensiveness about his use of Scots and a desire to gain the indulgence of a genteel audience. The volume is dedicated 'To the most Beautiful, the Scots Ladies', with a quotation from Prior to the effect that he writes only for the young and fair. But writing for the young and fair with the social assurance of a Prior is a very different matter from writing vigorous vernacular poems about ale-wives and brothel-keepers in a spirit of male conviviality, a mode in which Ramsay was particularly successful. Clearly, Ramsay's position was confused, and his view of his own role in Scottish culture kept shifting.

Ramsay's best known work is *The Gentle Shepherd*, a Scottish pastoral comedy written in a somewhat anglicized Scots interspersed with Scots songs some of which have genuine freshness and charm in the folk tradition. The play itself, with its somewhat clumsily contrived plot set against a simple background of rustic life and labour, manages, especially in its earlier scenes, to suggest by its language something of the true rhythms of agricultural labour, but the whole work is very precariously balanced, and several times falls into sentimentality, melodrama, or absurdity. Ramsay is hovering uneasily between a faded literary convention and an awareness of contemporary rustic life in the Scotland he knew, and has no sure method of linking the convention with the awareness. The result is an interesting if only partially successful balancing feat which reflects the unstable equilibrium of Scottish literary culture at this period.

Ramsay's work as an editor shows his Scottish interests more single-mindedly than his original poetry. *The Tea-Table Miscellany*, published in four volumes between 1724 and 1737, is a collection of songs and ballads, the first of many such in eighteenth-century Scotland. Some of the songs have been re-written in neo-classic English, others have been 'improved' in a variety of ways, others again are printed from broadside or other sources as Ramsay found them. In *The Ever Green*, published in 1724, Ramsay introduced his readers to the great poetry of late medieval Scotland, that of Dunbar and Henryson in particular. Most of this he took from the Bannatyne Manuscript, that invaluable anthology of earlier Scottish poetry compiled by George Bannatyne in 1568. Ramsay alters the text as it suits him, changing spelling, word order, and even stanza form where he felt this would make a poem more acceptable to his readers, and sometimes

re-phrasing a passage completely if he himself cannot understand the original. Sometimes he adds stanzas of his own, with
a sublime indifference to the enormous disparity in quality
between his own mock-antique Scots and the real thing. Two
fiercely patriotic poems are attributed to Alexander Scott but
are clearly by Ramsay himself. One laments the oppression of
Scotland by England and prophesies a successful fight for the
re-establishment of an independent kingdom of Scotland.
This is set in 1300, at the height of the Scottish war of
independence against England. It is significant that Ramsay
dared not speak in his own person when attacking the
Union and preaching Scottish independence. Scottish
nationalism in the eighteenth century inevitably became
associated with antiquarianism.

The preface to *The Ever Green* makes clear Ramsay's
patriotic intention: 'When these good old *Bards* wrote, we
had not yet made Use of imported Trimming upon our
Cloaths, nor of foreign Embroidery in our Writings. Their
Poetry is the product of their own Country, not pilfered and
spoiled in the Transportation from abroad: Their *Images* are
native, and their *Landskips* domestick; copied from those
Fields and Meadows we every Day behold'. This was written
by the same writer who imitated Pope and quoted Prior and
read the *Spectator* in order to model his life on the way of life
there indicated.

Ramsay was indeed a mixed and confused character.
Perhaps I may be allowed to quote a summing up of his
literary personality which I wrote for another occasion.
'Isaac Bickerstaff and Gavin Douglas; a gentleman of the
Augustan Age and an ardent Scottish patriot; an admirer of
Pope and Gay and Matthew Prior and a devoted champion of
the older Scottish makars and of the use of vernacular Scots by

contemporary Scottish poets; a seeker after polish and good breeding and a vulgar little gossip whose schoolboy snigger spoils many of his poems and songs; a sentimental Jacobite and a prudent citizen who cannily absented himself from Edinburgh when Prince Charlie held court in Holyrood in 1745; a champion of Scottish folk-song and a wrecker of scores of such songs by turning them into stilted would-be neo-classic effusions—the dualism in Ramsay's life and character was deep-seated and corresponded to a dualism in the Scottish culture of his day. He could defend the coarsest and frankest language in poetry and yet dress up a Scottish song in intolerable false elegancies. At the same time he could demonstrate that he possessed the Horatian elegance of the English gentleman by rendering Horace's "Vides ut alta stet nive candidum" in vivid and homely Scots verse.'[18]

Ramsay's collecting of Scots songs for *The Tea-Table Miscellany* was part of a growing interest in native Scottish airs which represented one of the principal ways in which eighteenth-century Scotland registered its national feeling. Manuscript anthologies of native airs arranged for a variety of instruments had already been made in Scotland throughout the seventeenth century, but the first printed collection of Scots airs for the voice appeared in 1725 under the title *Orpheus Caledonius*. Here William Thomson fitted simple but adequate basses to tunes that were often obscured by a profusion of ornaments; the taste of the age was already reflected in the shape of the tunes and in their accompaniments. They doubtless satisfied the public demand but they also helped to consolidate the tradition of genteel improving of

[18] 'Eighteenth-Century Vernacular Poetry', by David Daiches, in *Scottish Poetry: A Critical Survey*, edited by James Kinsley (London, 1955).

native products for the export market. *Orpheus Caledonius* was published in London; the words of its songs were often Ramsay's. In *The Tea-Table Miscellany*, while Ramsay did not print the music, he made it clear that these were songs meant to be sung. The titles of Ramsay's songs are the titles of the old popular tunes; the words, as I have noted, are printed with varying degrees of alteration: sometimes only the chorus is old and the rest new. The *Miscellany* includes—I give the titles as Ramsay prints them—'Lady Anne Bothwell's Lament' (which Watson had also printed), 'John Ochiltree', 'Todlen butt, todlen ben' (better known as 'Toddlen hame'), a version of 'Over the hills and far away', 'Rare Willy drown'd in Yarrow', 'Katherine Ogie', 'Sweet William's Ghost', 'Bonny Barbara Allan', 'The bonny Earl of Murray', 'Johnny Faa, the Gypsy Laddie', and very many more. Sometimes Ramsay's own words kept alive an air for which the original words had been lost and which might otherwise have perished. Sometimes he has several sets of words to the same air, as 'The Broom of Cowden-knows'. It is exasperating to find the song 'Tweedside' represented by such words as these:

> What beauties does Flora disclose?
>   How sweet are her smiles upon Tweed?
> Yet Mary's still sweeter than those;
>   Both nature and fancy succeed . . .

And it is saddening to find that it is these insipid words—by one Robert Crawford, who wrote several sets of similar words to other popular Scottish airs—that appear as 'Tweedside' in the subsequent song-collections of eighteenth-century Scotland. It is hard to forgive Ramsay for perpetuating such texts. For 'Logan Water' he has the following:

29

Tell me, Hamilla, tell me why
  Thou dost from him that loves thee run?
Why from his soft embraces fly,
  And all his kind endearments shun.

This is not to say that all songs in elegant neo-classic English are bad; but Ramsay's basic uncertainty of taste— his odd combination of anglicizing gentility and rustic Scottishness—was responsible for his perpetuating throughout the eighteenth century a great number of feeble and even preposterous words to old popular Scottish airs. Nevertheless, many of Ramsay's texts are sound, or as sound as he could make them by depending on broadside versions or even oral tradition.

Ramsay's own songs are at their best when he sticks to the folk idiom and enters with spirit into the atmosphere of the original refrain. 'An thou wert my ain thing' is on the whole well done, and so is the fine, lilting 'The widow can bake, the widow can brew'. Among his successful reworkings of old folk-songs are 'The Carle he came o'er the Croft', 'This is no my ain Hoose' and 'Clout the Cauldron'.

The *Orpheus Caledonius* was followed by a stream of similar publications of songs with music in Scotland. The most famous and the most complete of these is James Johnson's *Scots Musical Museum*, of which the first volume appeared in 1787 and to whose later volumes Burns contributed so much. As in the *Orpheus Caledonius*, each tune— and there are six hundred of them in the collection—is provided with a simple figured-bass accompaniment. Between Ramsay and Burns many songs were written to old and new tunes, some imitating the folk idiom, others in the style of English genteel songs of the time. Lady Grizel Baillie's imitation of the ballad style, 'Werena my heart licht I wad dee', was first printed in *The Tea-Table Miscellany* and appeared also in the *Orpheus Caledonius*. Lady Wardlaw's 'Hardyknute' passed as a genuine old ballad throughout much of the century. And there were very many more, often written by amateurs who wrote only a few songs or even only one. They include 'There's nae luck about the house', 'O weel may the boatie row', 'Logie o' Buchan', 'The Drunken Wife of Gallowa' (also known as 'Hoolie and Fairly') and others. Dance tunes, new and old, were fitted with words; 'Scotch airs' with all the obvious Scottish characteristics were composed; the pastoral, the genteel, and the folk inter-mingled in all sorts of ways.

Henry Mackenzie, who was born in 1745, looking back on the Edinburgh of his youth, remembered the immense popularity of singing.

My father was a remarkably good singer, and during some of our journeys used to hum some airs, his favorites, which now swell my bosom and almost draw tears from my eyes. Such was the air called *Gilderoy* now sung to the words, 'When first I saw thee graceful move'; *Lochaber no more*; *My apron dearie*, modernized in the words of Sir Gilbert Elliot . . . to the words, 'Why left I Aminta, why broke I my vow'; and *The Flowers of the Forest* . . . .

The ladies of Edinburgh used to sing those airs without any accompaniment (indeed they scarce admitted of counterpoint, or any but a slight and delicate accompaniment) at tea and after supper, their position at table not being interrupted as now by rising to the pianoforte.[19]

The most impressive eighteenth-century collection of songs—but of the words only—was that of David Herd, zealous antiquary and honest and modest collector whose two volumes published in 1776 brought together all the words,

[19] *The Anecdotes and Egotisms of Henry Mackenzie*, edited by Harold Wm. Thompson (London, 1927), p. 79.

new and old, of Scottish song that survived. It is a magnificent haul, including a section of what he called 'heroic ballads and fragments', with 'Johnny Armstrong', 'Bonny Barbara Allan', 'The Bonny Earl of Murray', 'Sir Patrick Spence', 'The Battle of Harlaw', and many others. (We must remember, as Herd well knew, that the ballads were meant to be sung.) There is a section of 'comic and humorous songs' and 'fragments of comic and humorous songs' which contains, in whole or in part, many—but alas far from all—of the originals which Ramsay and others had 'improved'. This section was to provide Burns with fragments and suggestions out of which he fashioned so many of the songs he sent to Johnson for his *Scots Musical Museum* and to George Thomson for his *Select Scottish Airs*. The very titles have a gusto about them—'Hey Jenny come doon to Jock', 'Todlen Hame', 'Here awa', there awa', 'Get up and bar the Door', 'Ranting roving lad' (also known as 'My love was born in Aberdeen'), 'When she came ben she bobbit', and many more. Herd was a great collector, and scrupulously faithful to the texts as he found them.

The eighteenth century in Scotland saw not only the publication of numerous collections of songs both with and without the music, but also collections of tunes alone, arranged for a variety of instruments. Many of these were dance tunes, some bearing the names of old songs of which the words had been lost. Some bore names suggesting that they might once have been songs, others have the names of dance tunes, almost always associated with particular people— Lady Charlotte Menzies Reel, Mr. Murray of Simprims Favourite, Miss Farquarson of Invercaulds Jig. Some of these dance tunes had been current in court, city and countryside for a hundred years and more; they had been speeded up in *tempo* and lost their words to become instrumental dance music. When Burns took some of these tunes, slowed down their *tempo*, and set words to them, he was unconsciously restoring them to something probably more like their earlier form.

The native dance tunes and song airs, so enormously popular in the middle of the century, were seriously threatened in the 1750s by the enthusiasm in Scotland for foreign, particularly Italian, music, and the current fashion for Italianizing Scottish airs. Names of Italian musicians begin to appear on the title-pages of collections of Scottish songs, and Italian music-teachers and singers became prominent in the teaching and performance of music in Edinburgh. Domenico Corri, Pietro Urbani, Giusto Ferdinando Tenducci, seem odd names to associate with the flourishing of the native air in Scotland. Tenducci was a singer who came to Edinburgh in 1768 to conduct concerts for the Musical Society. He produced and sang in two operas in Edinburgh in 1769, for which Robert Fergusson, then just beginning his sadly brief poetic career, wrote several songs to Scottish airs. Soon after, the poet and the singer quarrelled, perhaps because Fergusson began to realize and to resent what Tenducci and his like were doing to Scottish music. It is significant that on 5 March 1772—fourteen months after Tenducci had departed abruptly from Edinburgh—there appeared in *The Weekly Magazine or Edinburgh Amusement* Fergusson's *Elegy on the Death of Scots Music*, which lamented the ousting of traditional Scottish music by 'sounds fresh sprung frae Italy'. This was not mere xenophobia on Fergusson's part. Pretentious settings, overloaded with trills and other prettifications, were destroying the native vigour and simplicity of Scots song. Burns was to see this as Fergusson had seen it, and in his

33

letters to Johnson and Thomson, the editors of the collections in which most of his songs appeared, he made it clear where he stood on the matter. Still, it is a reflection of the impoverishment of Scottish culture that the issue should have been between a native simplicity and an imported sophistication: older Scottish polyphonic music, which died after the migration of the Court to England in 1603, had been fruitfully responsive to continental influence.

The over-elaborate arrangement of simple Scottish airs was only one aspect of a phenomenon common enough in eighteenth-century Scottish culture—national pride in the native heritage accompanied by a nervous desire to do the genteel thing. Fergusson and Burns were not the only ones who deplored this nervous defensiveness. The movement to prettify Scottish popular music goes back at least as far as Alexander Munro's *Collection of the Best Scots Songs* published in Paris in 1732—even earlier in English publications; but later editors sometimes resisted this tendency. William McGibbon, for example, an able Edinburgh musician and distinguished violinist, resisted the temptation to change the character of the old tunes in his three-volume *Collection of Scots Tunes* (1742 to 1755), and at the very end of the century John Watlen, an English music publisher settled in Edinburgh, brought out a *Complete Collection of Scots Songs* arranged, as he put it, 'plain and simple, without being Italianized in the least', in a vain attempt to turn the tide in the capital against the popularity of Corri and Urbani and their like.

A factor working in the other direction was the impact of the Jacobite movement on Scottish sensibility, once the cause was well and truly hopeless and the appeal of a lost cause could be combined with a nostalgic sense of a dwindled nationhood. 'Sentimental Jacobitism' brought an unsophisticated folk emotion back into Scottish song long after it had disappeared from other European countries. Burns himself drew on this emotion for some of his best songs, particularly where he associated with the lost Jacobite cause love and exile. In 'It was a' for our rightfu' king' he could even make a fine folk song out of an inferior street ballad, thus reversing the trend of normal development. The Jacobite movement brought a new surge of song to Scotland; some of it springing up anonymously, some adaptations of earlier popular songs, some, like Burns's, cunning imitations or completions of true folk song, some by minor versifiers who sometimes caught the genuine spark because of the kind of tradition which the after-math of the Jacobite movement brought into being. But this tradition soon dwindled down into facile sentimentality to join the other streams which flowed into the torrent of tartanry which increased steadily throughout the nineteenth century. If the Union of 1707 made possible a special kind of Scottish national feeling, it also created conditions which restricted its effective working in Scottish culture.

II. National Institutions: The Church and the Law

We are so accustomed to the association of Jacobitism with Scottish nationalism, and to the citing of the 'auld alliance' between Scotland and France as representing the traditional Scottish national posture, that we tend to forget that for a considerable period of time Scottish national feeling was Protestant and anti-French. I discussed in my last lecture the paradox involved in the eighteenth-century identification of Jacobitism and Scottish independence. We can see that paradox more clearly when we remember that it was Queen Mary's marriage to the Dauphin of France in 1558 and the acceptance of her husband as King Francis of Scotland that led many Scotsmen to feel that Scottish independence was being sacrificed to French interests. It was this feeling that precipitated the Reformation in Scotland. The Scottish Protestants ousted Mary of Guise, French and Catholic, from her position as regent late in 1559; she died soon after, and the government passed into the hands of the Lords of the Congregation who were responsible for the Scottish Parliament of 1560. It was this Parliament that overthrew Catholicism and enacted a Protestant Confession of Faith, although its acts never received royal approval.

There is yet another paradox here. The Scottish Parliament until very near the end of its life was far from a popular assembly: it was essentially feudal and baronial, and even though the lesser barons established their right to be present in 1560—thus strengthening the Protestant influence—it can hardly be said that Scotland's history-making Reformation Parliament represented the Scottish people. Nevertheless, the influence of Protestantism in Scotland was anti-feudal and in some directions revolutionary. The Reformation in Scotland as elsewhere 'tended to become the cause of the middle class, the lairds and burgesses, and awaken something more than preoccupations with monopolies and vested interests. It crossed feudal barriers and feudal ties, and drew the protestant nobles into a movement which feudalism could never hope to dominate.'[1] But it did more than this: it drew together in a common creed and a common outlook on life the small urban middle class of Scotland and those in country areas associated with them, to give them a political and, for a much longer period, a social influence out of proportion to their actual numbers. Further, the Parliament of 1560 though enthusiastic for the Reformation was not enthusiastic about John Knox's *First Book of Discipline*, which it rejected, the nobles being more concerned to get hold of church lands than to enact a stringent scriptural code which at the same time provided for the turning over of church lands to the reformed church. For seven years after this Parliament Knox's ecclesiastical views were denied formal political establishment, with the result that during this period Knox's Calvinism and Knox's form of discipline and of church government were practised voluntarily by those who believed in them, thus stamping Scottish Calvinism with a quality it was long to preserve. The

[1] *England and Scotland, 1560–1707*, by Douglas Nobbs (London, 1952), p. 34.

fourth head of the *First Book of Discipline* stated that 'it appertaineth to the people and to every several congregation to elect their own minister', who was to be examined in public. The fifth head related to the provision for the ministers and the distribution of the rents and possessions of the church, and also laid down that every church situated in a town of any size was to have a schoolmaster attached to it, while in every large town there was to be a college for teaching the arts and languages. The eighth head provided that elders and deacons should be chosen yearly in each congregation; the elders were to assist the minister in church affairs and in admonishing licentious livers, and were also to pay close attention to the life, manners, diligence, and study of the minister himself, to admonish and correct him, and even if necessary depose him.[2] The trust in the faithful layman shown here is extraordinary, and during the few years of the voluntary operation of this system helped to establish a deep democratic trend in Scottish Calvinism. There is a paradox here, too; for the democracy applied only to the faithful, and could and frequently did go together with the fiercest intolerance of all others. Still, a tradition of democracy, however drastic its limitations, and a tradition of popular education, however theoretical, left their mark on the Scottish church. Further, the movement of power and responsibility up from the local Kirk Session to the General Assembly, the supreme decision-making body of the church, provided for a transmission of opinion from outlying parts to the centre, confirmed the importance of the layman in the church and established a forum for the expression and the moulding of popular opinion that the Scottish Parliament had never been or claimed to be. All this is to be remembered

[2] *Ecclesiastical History of Scotland*, by George Grub (Edinburgh, 1861), vol. ii, pp. 93–95.

when we consider the consequences of the fact that the Union of 1707 left Scotland her national church.

To jump from 1560 to 1707, thus passing over the religious and political conflicts of the seventeenth century, is not to suggest that the Church of Scotland as it found itself in 1707 was identical with that envisaged by John Knox in 1560 or even with the presbyterianism officially established in Scotland in 1592 from which it was directly descended. This is not the place to trace the conflicts between episcopacy and presbytery, the relations between Scottish presbyterianism and English puritanism, the significance of the National Covenant of 1638 and the Solemn League and Covenant of 1643, or to tell the story of the church in Scotland under the Commonwealth and under the last two Stuart kings, or present an account of the ups and downs of presbyterianism as the established form of church government in Scotland before its official and final re-establishment after the Glorious Revolution in 1690. In that year those who survived of the anti-episcopal ministers ejected in 1662 were brought back, many episcopalian ministers having already been rudely expelled by the Cameronian rabble, and an act was passed ratifying and establishing the Confession of Westminster and establishing the presbyterian form of church government and discipline, viz., presbyteries, provincial synods, and general assemblies, as formerly recognized by the statute of 1592, except with regard to patronage, a consideration of which was reserved[3]—to precipitate some highly significant conflicts later. This religious settlement of 1690 deliberately ignored the extreme claims to be superior to the civil power that the Covenanters had made in their headier moments; indeed, it passed over the Covenants altogether and did not

[3] ibid., vol. iii, p. 305.

39

repeal the 1662 act which condemned them. The oath of allegiance replaced any religious test as the passport to political office, and excommunication was deprived of its civil penalties.[4]

Now it is doubtless true, as Douglas Nobbs has put it, that 'the establishment of presbyterianism closed the struggle over divine right in church and state. From 1690, the General Assembly met annually and exercised the greatest influence on the nation. The presbyterian ideal of the co-operation of the civil and ecclesiastical powers had triumphed at the same time that a limited monarchy had ended the claims of the prerogative.'[5] At the same time, we must recognize that no settlement could have succeeded in institutionalizing in a satisfactory national form all the ideals, aspirations, beliefs, and principles which had been developed in the fierce religious and politico-religious conflicts of the preceding century. These conflicts had built religious principle into the national character, in the Lowlands at least, in a very special way. Religion was associated in different ways by different groups with freedom, nationality, and in some cases with class feeling against social and economic superiors, as well as with the kingdom of God and the rule of the elect on earth. In some respects strong Calvinist feeling was reactionary, as when it led to farmers refusing any kind of modernization of agricultural methods on the grounds that God's will must not be interfered with. Those who accept in too simplified a form the Weber-Tawney thesis about Protestantism and capitalism might ponder the significance of a letter written by a Glasgow merchant to a merchant in Edinburgh in 1724: 'You seem to be most uneasy about the misfortunes of a bad market and do

---

[4] *Scotland and the Union, 1695–1747*, by William Law Mathieson (Glasgow, 1905), p. 14.   [5] op. cit., pp. 158–9.

not submit yourself to the providence of a Divine hand which orders all things as He seeth meet. You seem to spurn against your disappointments. You are to make the best of a bad market. You can, which we see is the fate of an honest dealer. Mercats is sometimes up and sometimes down.'[6] Belief in predestination is not easily reconciled with belief in the necessity of controlling events by purposive action, nor is the Calvinist belief in a tiny minority of those predestined to be saved, by God's grace and not by any acts of their own, amid the vast majority of the predestinate damned, logically related either to progressive or to charitable actions.

Calvinism denied freedom of the will, yet the way in which Calvinist prebyterianism emerged in Scotland associated it, in some quarters at least, with an idea of national freedom and also with an idea of democracy. A member of the elect was bound by no external authority, but only by his own inner sense of God's will and his own reading of the Scriptures. Yet on the other hand the chain of authority from the Kirk Session up to the General Assembly was recognized as the channel through which God's will for His church was to be interpreted. In other words, Calvinism forced the responsibility on to the individual elect while presbyterianism assigned it to the General Assembly. What happened when the individual and the Assembly disagreed? Scottish ecclesiastical history gives the answer clearly: disruption.

The paradox of the co-existence of a belief in individual freedom and extreme intolerance meets us at every turn in Scottish ecclesiastical history. In 1695 the Scottish Parliament ratified an older act making blasphemy a capital offence,

---

[6] *An Economic History of Scotland in the Eighteenth Century*, by Henry Hamilton (Oxford, 1963), p. xiv. (From the Papers of Robert Harris, Merchant, Edinburgh, 1718–32.)

and the following year the General Assembly, in a warning against Deism, equated it with atheism. In January 1697 Thomas Aikenhead, a twenty-year-old student, was hanged at Edinburgh on the evidence of a single fellow student who said that he had heard him declare Christ to be an impostor, even though Aikenhead himself first denied the charge then, when this proved useless, confessed and repented. Even his plea for a short reprieve was refused. The ministers of the Church of Scotland 'spoke and preached for cutting him off'.[7] Ministers themselves, if they deviated from the ruthless logic of Calvinism in favour of natural religion or humane reason in any degree, were rebuked or suspended. Nevertheless, as the eighteenth century advanced the intellectual and theological climate changed somewhat. When John Simson, Professor of Divinity at Glasgow, was accused in the General Assembly of 1714 of teaching Arminianism, much argument but no drastic action ensued. This moderating of extremist opinion and action was already foreshadowed in the career of William Carstares, King William's chief adviser on Scottish affairs, Principal of Edinburgh University from 1703 to 1715 and leader of the Church of Scotland until his death in the latter year: Carstares, a subtle politician, both bowed to popular extremist opinion and found many indirect ways of guiding it. Without yielding an inch in his stern religious convictions, he was able to ensure that the Scottish church as it moved from the period of the Glorious Revolution to that of the Union contained within itself the possibility of adapting to new circumstances.

A much bigger step in the direction of moderating extremist opinion and intolerance in the Church of Scotland was marked by the appointment of the humane moralist, William Leech-

---

[7] Mathieson, op. cit., p. 221.

man, a pupil of Francis Hutcheson, to the chair of Divinity at Glasgow in 1743, and the unsuccessful attempt to prosecute him for his views on prayer. But most of all is the process evident in the careers of the two William Wisharts, father and son, both of whom held office as Principal of Edinburgh University. The elder Wishart was five times Moderator of the General Assembly, and gave offence to the unco guid by his genial humanity, while the younger was in the habit of using the prayer: 'Lord rebuke and bear down a spirit of imposition and persecution, not only in Papists, but in Christians of whatever denomination.'[8]

Nevertheless, the movement of the Church of Scotland in the eighteenth century towards what is known as Moderatism is far from being the whole story. The church had to bear some of the responsibilities of a lost nationhood, and it was not adequately equipped to do so. In spite of its zeal for education, one could hardly look to it to provide patronage for the arts. And this was something desperately needed in Scotland. Ever since the removal of court patronage in 1603 Scotland lacked a focus for literature and the arts; the time had passed for a Great House culture, even if the economy of Scotland could have supported it (though it must be admitted that some great houses preserved musical and literary documents, and others throughout the eighteenth and early nineteenth centuries served in some degree as literary centres).[9] Of the two national institutions left to Scotland after 1707, the church was by its history and its doctrine prevented from supplying this lack; the law was more successful, but worked within inevitable limitations. If we add the burghs as a third possible

[8] ibid., p. 258.
[9] *Scottish Literature and the Scottish People 1680–1830*, by David Craig (London, 1961), Appendix A: 'Scottish Great Houses as Literary Centres'.

source of patronage, while it is true that they did something for education and that after the Reformation the old sang-schools, once under the cathedrals, came under the aegis of the burghs, we do not find them of much help in the eighteenth century.

The strong opposition of the church to the establishment of a theatre in Scotland was only one of many indications of its unfitness to be a champion of the arts. When John Home's moral and sentimental tragedy *Douglas* was acted in Edinburgh in 1756, the outcry from the orthodox or 'high flyers' was tremendous, even though by this time Moderatism was well established in the city. Alexander Carlyle, minister of Inveresk, who attended the performance on the third night, was prosecuted by the Presbytery of Dalkeith; Thomas Whyte, minister of Liberton, submitted to a six weeks' suspension for having attended the play, his sentence being thus mitigated because, though he did attend, he tried to conceal himself behind a pillar. Home himself withdrew from the church.[10] But Moderate opinion, in Edinburgh at least, was in the ascendant, and Carlyle tells us that 'in the year 1784, when the great actress Mrs. Siddons first appeared in Edinburgh, during the sitting of the General Assembly, that court was obliged to fix all its important business for the alternate days when she did not act, as all the younger members, clergy as well as laity, took their stations in the theatre on those days by three in the afternoon'.[11]

It would be wrong, however, to see this issue as represent-

[10] *The Autobiography of Alexander Carlyle of Inveresk* (Edinburgh, 1910), pp. 325 ff.

[11] ibid., pp. 338–9. But the change had not apparently taken place by 1776. 'The Clergy are expected to go to no public place whatever: a Play, in particular, however innocent or sentimental, is esteemed highly immoral for a Minister; and were he once to be seen at an Assembly, he might as well resign his profession; for no one would listen to him afterwards.' *Letters from Edinburgh, written in the years 1774 and 1775* [by Capt. Edward Topham] (London, 1776), p. 237.

ing a straight fight between civilization and the arts, represented by the Moderates, and bigotry and narrowness represented
by the High Flyers. John Home was no Shakespeare, in spite
of patriotic Scottish claims that he was Shakespeare's equal,
and the facile deism which so many of the Moderates
opposed to the orthodox was a pretty shallow creed. Those
ministers of the Church of Scotland who were members of the
Edinburgh *literati*—William Robertson, Hugh Blair,
Thomas Blacklock, and others—were neither profound
thinkers, great imaginative writers, nor brilliant literary
critics. Robertson was in his way an accomplished historian,
Hugh Blair a rhetorical critic of some historical interest, and
Dr. Blacklock a poetaster who accurately reflected the
genteel taste of his day. But none of them, and indeed none of
the *literati* except David Hume, possessed either the imaginative genius that would provide a focus for a literary revival or
the philosophic depth and subtlety to construct an intellectual
position that could vie with Calvinism in strength and logic
and provide an alternative philosophy of life. Hume, whose
greatness as a philosopher was not understood by his Scottish
contemporaries, was content to live in Edinburgh in an
atmosphere of cultured geniality, associating on the most
cordial terms with those Moderates whose intellectual
position his philosophy, had they only known it, had completely undermined.

It might be considered unfair to ask that a national church
should also be considered as a potential focus for a national
culture, but the circumstances under which the Church of
Scotland was left as one of the country's two surviving national
institutions after 1707 demand that we consider it in this
light. While there can be no doubt that the church did
canalize some streams of Scottish national feeling and while it

is true also that the General Assembly played a more significant part in Scottish life and thought than the Scottish
Parliament had done, at least until its last few years, it is
equally true that neither High Flyers nor Moderates could
give significant cultural meaning to the religious aspirations
of the Scottish people. The religious debates of eighteenth-
century Scotland in the end provided literature only with the
kind of pawky anecdotes about ministers that Dean Ramsay
used in his *Reminiscences of Scottish Life and Character* in
1858 and that Barrie was to exploit in his Thrums stories.
Only James Hogg's *Private Memoirs and Confessions of a
Justified Sinner* (1824) makes real imaginative literary use of
Calvinism, though Robert Louis Stevenson showed some
signs of also being able to do so. This is not to say that
puritanism, of the Scottish or any other variety, is necessarily
inimical to art; there were signs of a Scottish puritan culture
in the late seventeenth century, of which the limited but
interesting work of William Cleland is one. And the literature
of New England shows what can be done with a puritan
tradition. But Scotland's national church in the eighteenth
century was too preoccupied to be free to help the literary
imagination.

The story of the various splits in the Scottish church shows
how great were the strains on it as a national church. There
were many serious controversies before any actual secession
took place—the controversy about the 'Auchterarder creed',
the controversy over Fisher's *Marrow of Modern Divinity*,
the controversy over Professor Simson's teaching already
referred to, the controversy over the abjuration oath, among
others. But most serious of all was the controversy about
patronage. When presbyterianism was restored in 1690 the
question of patronage—i.e. on who actually decides on the

appointment of a minister—was reserved; the decision was subsequently left in the hands of the heritors and elders in the country and the magistrates and elders in a town, with a right of appeal to the presbytery. But in 1712 an act passed the Commons restoring the right of presentation to patrons (the traditional owners of the right of presentation, through property ownership or some other qualification) if they had not actually renounced it; only if the patron did not present within six months would the right pass to the presbytery. (Of course Roman Catholic patrons as well as those suspected of political disloyalty were debarred. Many livings were in the gift of the Crown.) Much argument ensued and many compromise proposals were suggested, and all the time the demand for the popular election of ministers grew among the more orthodox especially in country districts unaffected by the rising tide of Moderatism, while among the landed gentry and in the cities more liberal views prevailed. Though there were significant exceptions, on the whole it can be said that the popular view was the narrower and the autocratic view the more enlightened—a paradox which resulted in considerable confusion and contradiction, particularly in the latter part of the century when democratic feeling and liberal theological views (as in Burns, for example) could force a man to take the anti-popular line on this question. The General Assembly in 1732 passed an act naming the heritors and elders as those responsible not merely for proposing but for actually electing and calling a minister to a parish, with the congregation consulted only after the process was over. This act was strongly opposed by Ebenezer Erskine, minister at Stirling, who preached a bitter sermon at the opening of the Synod of Perth and Stirling attacking the General Assembly's decision. The synod rebuked him, the rebuke was confirmed by the

General Assembly of 1733, and Erskine and three fellow ministers wrote a strong protest against the rebuke which they declined to withdraw. Appeals to compromise failed, and in 1734 the four ministers formed themselves into an Associate Presbytery. The Associate Presbytery became the Associate Synod in 1742, which itself split in 1747 on the question of the 'burgher oath'—i.e. whether it was proper for them to take an oath to uphold 'the true religion presently professed within this realm' which might be construed as condoning the corruptions of the established church. The two groups became known as the Burgher Synod and the Anti-Burgher Synod.[12] They were not reunited until 1827.

The Burgher Synod later itself split (on the question of civil compulsion in religious matters) into Original Burghers and Burghers, popularly known as Auld Lichts and New Lichts. A more gentle secession was that led by Thomas Gillespie, originating in a dispute about patronage: in 1761 Gillespie and Thomas Boston, whose popular election to the parish of Jedburgh had been over-ruled by the Crown and the heritors and magistrates, together founded the Relief Church 'for the relief of Christians oppressed in their Christian privileges'. Yet another group had been founded in 1730 by John Glas, who deplored the legalism of the Presbyterian establishment: the Glassites saw the true church of the New Testament as simply a group of congregations united in brotherly love, 'subject to no jurisdiction under Heaven'. They gave each other the kiss of greeting and made much of social occasions.

What are we to conclude from this hectic story of perpetual

[12] The clearest short account of the business will be found in Mathieson, op. cit., chapter VII. See also the same author's *The Awakening of Scotland, 1747–97* (Glasgow, 1910), chapter IV, and *Social Life in Scotland in the Eighteenth Century*, by H. Gray Graham (London, 1899), vol. ii, chapter IX.

splitting among those who took religion seriously going on side by side with the steady rise of a Moderatism which stood for polite letters and a genteel culture? That the Union of 1707 forced on Scottish religion a role which it was unable to bear? Perhaps; but we have to go to the end of this particular chapter before we can see the true picture. As the eighteenth century came to an end the Moderates became more and more associated with power, respectability, and worldliness. They ceased to represent, in the eyes of an increasing number of people, any genuinely religious or any genuinely Scottish feeling at all. An evangelical revival at the beginning of the nineteenth century brought the question of patronage to the forefront once again. In 1837 the Court of Session ruled that the presentation of a candidate who had been rejected by the Presbytery of Auchterarder, on the grounds that a majority of the responsible parishioners objected, was nevertheless valid, and the House of Lords upheld this decision in 1839. Further cases of the same kind followed, and the General Assembly came into direct conflict with the government on the whole issue of patronage. The crash—as Lord Cockburn called it— came in the General Assembly in June 1843. The Moderates were for the government, the evangelicals against. Dr. Welsh, the previous year's Moderator of the General Assembly, opened the proceedings with a protest, and then walked out with a large number of ministers and elders, to form the Free Church of Scotland under the leadership of Thomas Chalmers. Here is Cockburn's vivid account of what happened:

They were joined outside by a large body of adherents, among whom were about 300 clergymen. As soon as Welsh, who wore his Moderator's dress, appeared on the street, and people saw that principle had really triumphed over interest, he and his followers were received with the loudest acclamations. They walked in procession down Hanover Street to Canonmills, where they had secured an excellent hall, through an unbroken mass of cheering people, and beneath innumerable handkerchiefs waving from the windows. But amidst this exultation there was much sadness and many a tear, many a grave face and fearful thought; for no one could doubt that it was with sore hearts that these ministers left the Church, and no thinking man could look on the unexampled scene and behold that the temple was rent, without pain and sad forebodings. No spectacle since the Revolution reminded one so forcibly of the Covenanters. . . .

For the present the battle is over. But the peculiar event that has brought it to a close is as extraordinary, and in its consequences will probably prove as permanent, as any single transaction in the history of Scotland, the Union alone excepted. The fact of above 450 clerical members of an Establishment, being above a third of its total complement, casting it off, is sufficient to startle any one who considers the general adhesiveness of Churchmen to their sect and their endowments. But when this is done under no bodily persecution, with no accession of power, from no political motive, but purely from dictates of conscience, the sincerity of which is attested by the sacrifice not merely of professional station and emoluments but of all worldly interests, it is one of the rarest occurrences in moral history. I know no parallel to it. There have been individuals in all ages who have defied and even courted martyrdom in its most appalling forms, but neither the necessity of such a fate nor its glory have been within the view of any one in modern times, and we must appreciate recent sacrifices in reference to the security of the age for which these clergymen were trained . . . They have abandoned that public station which was the ambition of their lives, and have descended from certainty to precariousness, and most of them from comfort to destitution, solely for their principles. And the loss of the stipend is the least of it. The dismantling of the manse, the breaking up of all the objects to which the hearts and the habits of the family were attached, the shutting of the gate for the last time of the little garden, the termination of all their interest in the humble but respectable kirk—even all these desolations, though they may excite the most immediate pangs, are not the calamities which the head of the house finds it hardest to sustain. It is the loss of station that is the deep and lasting sacrifice, the ceasing to be the most important man in the parish, the closing of the doors of the gentry against him and his family, the altered prospects of his children, the extinction of everything that the State had provided for the decent dignity of the manse and its inmates. . . .

. . . What similar sacrifice has ever been made in the British empire? Among what other class, either in Scotland or in England, could such a proceeding have occurred? The doctors? the lawyers? Oxford? the English Church? the Scotch lairds? It is the most honourable fact for Scotland that its whole history supplies. The common sneers at the venality of our country, never just, are now absurd.[13]

I have quoted at length from this account by a contemporary, because it stresses an aspect of the Disruption which is very relevant to my argument. Cockburn saw it as Scotland's last heroic act. It seems to me to represent— whatever else it may also represent—the last attempt by the church in Scotland to act out the national role forced on it, one might almost say, by the Union of 1707. Throughout the eighteenth and early nineteenth centuries Scotland had no true political life of its own; it was 'managed' by an appointee of the government in London, and never more so than during the long reign of 'King Harry IX', Henry Dundas, Viscount Melville, who was in complete control of Scottish affairs from 1782 until after the turn of the century. The church, through the General Assembly, remained the voice of at least one large part of Scotland; and when that voice became simply the echo of a spineless establishment another voice made itself heard. The evangelical party in the Scottish church in the early nineteenth century may have been narrow in all sorts of ways, but it acted to prove not only that Moderatism was not enough but also that there was still one field left for the assertion of a Scottish individuality.

[13] *Journal of Henry Cockburn, 1831–1854* (Edinburgh, 1874), vol. ii, pp. 21–32.

If the Church of Scotland kept splitting from within because it could not adequately sustain the role forced on it by the consequences of the Union, it must be remembered that outside the established church there were religious traditions that claimed to be more thoroughly national and more adequately linked with Scotland's past. The Reformation in Scotland, unlike the English Reformation, did not seek and find a deliberate compromise between tradition and reform of the kind represented by Queen Elizabeth's Thirty-nine Articles. It broke more violently with the country's religious past, leaving to the Catholics the boast of continuity. Catholics, of course, remained in Scotland in spite of the Parliament of 1560 and the subsequent violent assertion of presbyterianism; in parts of the Highlands, in particular in parts of the north-west and the Western Islands, there were considerable Catholic communities. In 1755 the Reverend Alexander Webster, minister of the Tolbooth Church, Edinburgh, produced in his *Account of the Number of People in Scotland in the Year One thousand Seven hundred & Fifty Five*[14] the first national census of Scotland. Unofficial and crude in method though this is, it does give us some indication of the extent and distribution of Scotland's population in the mid-eighteenth century, and as it also divides the inhabitants into 'Papists' and 'Protestants' it gives us an idea of the relative numbers of each, even though one suspects that the number of Papists has been minimized. Webster shows a total of 1,248,890 Protestants and 16,490 Papists. 2,288 Papists are shown in Aberdeenshire (beside 113,800 Protestants), compared with 263 in the county of Edinburgh

[14] A manuscript copy of this work, preserved in the Advocates Library, Edinburgh (now the National Library of Scotland), was copied in cyclostyle by the Registrar General of Scotland in 1921 and circulated to a few interested people. I have used one of these copies.

or Midlothian. 'The Papists who reside in Edinburgh', remarks Webster in a note, 'being generally Persons in low life such as Chairmen &c. their precise number cannot be ascertained but they will at least amount to the number stated.' These 'persons in low life' were largely Highlanders who had come to the city to take such jobs as they could find. 5,664 Papists are shown in Inverness-shire (exclusive of Skye); of these 2,040 were in South Uist and Benbecula, 2,416 in Harris, 1,100 in Barra, and 827 in Glenelg. There were clearly whole Catholic communities in these areas. Elsewhere, even in the Highlands they were very scattered: Ross-shire had only twenty in all. Banffshire on the other hand had 3,150, of whom 843 were in Inneraven, 822 in Rathven, 431 in Kirkmichael (over half the inhabitants), 540 in Bellie, 233 in Huntly, and 75 in Mortlach.

But more important politically and culturally in the eighteenth century than the Catholics were the Episcopalians, who after all had represented the established form of Protestantism in Scotland for a considerable part of the seventeenth century. We are so accustomed to reading of the fight of Scottish Presbyterians against the imposition of Anglican forms—the bitter struggle against bishops and against 'Laud's Liturgy'—that we may forget that a considerable number of Scotsmen saw in Episcopalianism a form of ecclesiastical organization and church worship which, while Protestant, linked them with their past and preserved the continuity of their history. It was in Episcopalian households that the older traditions of music and poetry were more likely to be preserved, especially in the north-east. John Skinner, minister at the Scottish Episcopal church of Langside, Aberdeenshire, was author of many rollicking songs and poems, including 'Tullochgorum', which Burns called 'the best Scotch song ever Scotland saw'. It was Skinner's son, also John Skinner, Bishop of Aberdeen from 1786 to his death in 1816, who obtained the repeal of the old penal statutes against Scottish Episcopalians in 1792. Previous to this, they had had a hard time. With the re-establishment of Presbyterianism in 1690 Episcopalian ministers who would not conform to the new régime were forced out of their livings, to find an often precarious livelihood where they could. Some continued to conduct services in private houses before small congregations, and though this was not itself illegal at the beginning of the eighteenth century, it could often lead to persecution, or to prosecution on a technicality. Adam Cockburn in Glasgow (popularly known as 'Amen' Cockburn, since the word 'Amen' was associated especially with Episcopalians) was attacked and driven out by the mob for using Episcopal forms and the English service—the latter gave particular offence. And there were similar cases. After the Jacobite Rebellion of 1715 and still more after the Forty-five, Episcopalianism became, with some reason, associated in the minds of the authorities with Jacobitism, and in 1736 and 1748 the laws against them were made much stiffer, so that it became almost impossible for an Episcopalian minister to conduct the most private and informal service before even a tiny handful of people. It was only after the Jacobite threat disappeared, and especially after the death of Prince Charlie in 1788, that the Episcopalian lot became easier.

The Episcopalian tradition in Aberdeenshire and else-where was a strongly Scottish one and satisfied some national instincts that the sterner Presbyterian tradition stifled. In the north generally Episcopalians and Catholics kept up Gaelic while Presbyterian ministers often tried to stamp it out. Scottish Episcopalians were more in touch with Scotland's medieval past than any Protestants in the covenanting tradition could possibly be. They bore no blame for the destruction of abbeys and churches and the suppressing of popular literature and festivities. Yet the Scottish Episcopalians were in no sense Scoto-catholic. Though some of them used the English service-book, most did not, at least in the earlier years of the century, depending on the Bible and on extempore prayer like any Covenanter, and wearing no surplice but a black gown. There was a simplicity about Scottish Episcopalian worship in the eighteenth century that is not generally associated with Episcopalian forms and was not wholly the result of the poverty of the Scottish Episcopal Church. They had no very specific theology, and had to profess only a faith in the Scriptures; it was only after 1792, by one of the provisions of the act repealing the penal statutes against them, that Scottish Episcopal ministers were required to subscribe to the Thirty-nine Articles.

The Scottish Episcopal Church in the eighteenth century thus possesses a certain charm—and charm is hardly a word that one would apply to any other religious group in Scotland at this time. There has been a modern trend towards rewriting Scottish political and ecclesiastical history in their favour, emphasizing not the persecution of the Covenanters by Laudians and Cavaliers but the bigotry and intolerance of the covenanting tradition as opposed to the greater human warmth and the greater links with tradition found in the Episcopalian way. The Scottish Episcopalian tradition has often had a greater appeal to literary men than the Presbyterian. Walter Scott joined the Scottish Episcopal Church for reasons given very precisely by Lockhart: 'He took up, early in life, a repugnance to the mode in which public worship is conducted in the Scottish Establishment; and adhered to the sister Church, whose system of government and discipline he believed to be the fairest copy of the primitive polity, and whose litanies and collects he reverenced as having been transmitted to us from the age immediately succeeding that of the Apostles'.[15] To Scott, always interested in the relation of the Scottish present with the Scottish past, the Scottish Episcopal Church maintained continuity with Scotland's past as the Church of Scotland, by the circumstances of its birth and early development, could not.

Besides its own national church, the Union of 1707 left Scotland its own national legal system. Edinburgh was a lawyers' city, containing both the Court of Session (the supreme court in civil causes, dating from 1532) and the High Court of Justiciary, which dealt with criminal cases and was founded only in 1672. The Court of Session sat in Parliament House; its fourteen judges—Senators of the College of Justice, also known as Lords of Session—were presided over by a fifteenth, the Lord President. Six of the Lords of Session constituted the bench of the High Court of Justiciary, presided over by the Lord Justice-Clerk, who was also one of the fifteen Lords of Session. These judges were 'law lords': i.e. on appointment they took the title of Lord X (e.g., Henry Home, Lord Kames; James Burnett, Lord Monboddo; Robert MacQueen, Lord Braxfield), but the title was not hereditary. Judges formed the apex of a legal community which itself formed an Edinburgh aristocracy. Peter Williamson's *Edinburgh Directory* for 1773-4 lists the citizens by rank in a somewhat surprising order: first come the Lords of Session, followed by Advocates, Writers to the Signet, Lords' and Advocates' Clerks, Physicians, Noble-

---

[15] *Memoirs of the Life of Sir Walter Scott, Bart.*, by J. G. Lockhart (Edinburgh, 1837), vol. vii, p. 414.

men and Gentlemen, Merchants, and so on.[16] The eighteenth-century Scot was a litigious character, and gave the legal profession plenty to do. Yet members of the profession were very active in general cultural pursuits, especially the historical and the antiquarian. A legal training was regarded as a good general education in Scotland well beyond the eighteenth century—Robert Louis Stevenson as well as Walter Scott was trained in the law. Many judges, advocates, and 'writers' regarded themselves, with varying degrees of conscious awareness, as guardians of a peculiarly Scottish tradition. They realized the national character of the Scottish legal system, and being an élite they regarded themselves as leaders not only of society but of national thought.

Thus the law in eighteenth-century Scotland was regarded not only as a profession leading to political advancement but also as a gentlemanly pursuit and a guarantee of a liberal mind. 'The Gentlemen who are styled Advocates in this country', wrote Captain Topham when he visited Edinburgh in 1745, 'are almost innumerable; for every man who has nothing to do, and no better name to give himself, is called Advocate. Of those, however, who practise and get business, the number is extremely few; but amongst these few, are some men whose abilities are not only an honour to the profession, but to the country itself: Men who make the bar a school of eloquence, and not, as I am sorry to say with us, a jargon of barbarous and almost unintelligible words, and who preserve, in their debates, the manners and sentiments of Gentlemen.'[17] Many of the *literati* were Lords of Session, especially after

[16] *A Scottish Man of Feeling*, by Harold William Thompson (London, 1931), pp. 34–35. 'Advocate' was (and is) the Scottish term for the English 'barrister'; Writers to the Signet were a very select body of solicitors or 'writers' as they were known in Scotland.

[17] *Letters from Edinburgh*, pp. 315–16.

the middle of the century. Sir Gilbert Elliot, Lord Minto, who was Lord Justice-Clerk from 1763 to 1766, is singled out by Ramsay of Ochtertyre as an important 'early promoter of polite literature in this country'. 'For many years', Ramsay continues, 'he was one of the *literati* to whose opinion much deference was paid by the authors of new works in verse or prose. Though too lazy, or too busy, to write anything himself, he was looked upon as a very judicious critic, whose taste might be relied on as likely to anticipate that of the public. Perhaps he was better acquainted with the *belles lettres* than with the quiddities of the feudal or municipal law'.[18] It is significant that so much of Ramsay's manuscript is concerned with legal characters, and that his discussion of literature and his discussion of the characters of judges tend to fall together. When he discusses a judge who has made no contribution to literature, he notes the fact wonderingly. 'Of the extent and nature of his literary knowledge', he remarks of Lord Drummore, 'it is difficult to speak. He wrote no books or even pamphlets that we know of.'[19] Of Charles Erskine, Lord Tinwald, Ramsay remarks:

Of the nature and extent of this gentleman's literature, and of his talents for composition, it is difficult to speak with precision. It may, however, be taken for granted that, educated as he was for college life, he laid in an ample store of knowledge, taken from the best books, ancient and modern. When an eminent counsel and a servant of the Crown, and still more when a judge, he had no time to increase his store, which, from all I could ever hear, was fully sufficient for every purpose. Be that as it may, he had all along a great name as man of taste; and the elegance and precision of his law papers were a strong proof that he had at an early period of life paid more attention to an innate style than most of his brethren in those days. They were for a great while considered as masterpieces in point of

[18] *Scotland and Scotsmen in the Eighteenth Century*, vol. i, p. 81.   [19] ibid., p. 99.

language. Every young lawyer, therefore, aspired at copying him in his manner of speaking and writing.[20]

I cite such comments not for the importance of the objective evaluation of the subject's literary skill which they reveal, but to indicate how much Ramsay, who was born in Edinburgh in 1736, son of a Writer to the Signet, took for granted that in discussing a man of law it was natural that one should mention his literary works and abilities. The comments made on judges who had no particular claim to literary fame are all the more revealing, for Ramsay feels that this lack is something requiring explanation.

It is significant that Scotland's great library was the Advocates' Library (now the National Library of Scotland): it was the lawyers who provided most of the researchers into Scotland's past. Sir David Dalrymple, who became a Lord of Session as Lord Hailes in 1766, was also historian, antiquary, editor, essayist, and general man of letters, author of the *Annals of Scotland* and *The Canons of the Church of Scotland*, editor of the Bannatyne Manuscript, contributor to Henry Mackenzie's periodical *The Mirror*, collector of ballads (in which activity he assisted Bishop Percy). A patriotic student of Scotland's historical and literary past, and at the same time a man of the world who had been educated at Eton and studied civil law at Utrecht, Lord Hailes represented the eighteenth-century Scottish ideal of a man of law. For the law in eighteenth-century Scotland represented at the same time a national inheritance, a standard of culture, and a social *élite*.

Henry Home, who became a Lord of Session as Lord Kames in 1752 and a Lord of Justiciary eleven years later, could perhaps be considered to possess an even greater claim than Lord Hailes to stand for the ideally cultivated Scottish

[20] ibid., pp. 105–6.

man of law of the period, and certainly his contemporaries regarded him rather in this light. But his interests were less strongly Scottish than those of Lord Hailes, his scholarship was more widely diffused and less profound and original, and his tone one of elegant common sense rather than careful research or inquiry. It may be true that, as Ramsay of Ochtertyre claimed, Lord Kames 'did more to promote the interests of philosophy and *belles lettres* in Scotland than all the men of law had done for a century together' and it is certainly true that, again in Ramsay's word 'he was an early and zealous cultivator of our arts and manufactures'.[21] And I have already referred to his zeal for agricultural improvement. Yet a period of time spent with Lord Kames's works produces a curious effect of having lived in a world of cotton wool. The smooth, discursive, intelligent yet never searching discourse gradually wears one down. 'In training young women, exhibite every thing to them in an agreeable light; and in particular, suffer them not to imagine that there can be any pain in doing what is right'.[22] 'Refinement of taste in a nation, is always accompanied with refinement of manners: people accustomed to behold order and elegance in public buildings and public gardens, acquire urbanity in private'.[23] 'In works exposed continually to public view, variety ought to be studied. It is a rule accordingly in sculpture, to contrast the different limbs of a statue, in order to give it all the variety possible. Though the cone in a single view be more beautiful than the pyramid; yet a pyramidal steeple, because of its variety, is justly preferred'.[24]

[21] *Scotland and Scotsmen in the Eighteenth Century*, vol. i, p. 179.
[22] *Loose Hints upon Education, chiefly concerning the Culture of the Heart* (Edinburgh, 1781), p. 140.
[23] *Sketches of the History of Man* (Edinburgh, 1813), vol. i, p. 172.
[24] *Elements of Criticism* (Dublin, 1762), vol. i, p. 241.

The tone of elegant rumination which characterizes Lord Kames's writings was not altogether matched by his personal behaviour. Ramsay of Ochtertyre refers to his 'levity or prurience of speech'[25] and there is other testimony to the raciness of his conversation. His favourite term, both of affection and reproach, applied to members of either sex, was 'bitch', and he once said of himself that 'I ken very weel that I am the coarsest and most black-a-vised bitch in a' the Court o' Session'. On his last visit to the Court, shortly before his death in his eighty-seventh year, he took farewell of his legal brethren with the exclamation, 'Fare ye a' weel, ye bitches!'[26] He was not, however, as hard a drinker as most of his colleagues, though, again in Ramsay's words, 'when he met with people to his liking that liked their bottle, he could occasionally drink hard'.[27] He had, in fact, his eccentricities, and there were few Lords of Session at this time who had none. The most notoriously eccentric was James Burnett, who took (from his Kincardineshire estate) the title of Lord Monboddo on becoming Lord of Session in 1767. Monboddo had much more solid learning than Kames, to whose superficiality he drew attention when, on being asked by Kames whether he had read his *Elements of Criticism*, he replied, 'No, my lord. You write much quicker than I can read'.[28] Monboddo is remembered for his belief that babies were born with tails and for his immoderate enthusiasm for ancient Greece, but though most of his theories are indeed odd, many are based both on learning and on genuine reflection and

[25] op. cit., vol. i, p. 213.
[26] *Kay's Edinburgh Portraits*, mostly written by James Paterson and edited by James Maidment (London and Glasgow, 1885), vol. i, p. 25.
[27] op. cit., vol. i, p. 213.
[28] *Lord Monboddo and Some of His Contemporaries*, by William Knight (London, 1900), p. 28.

some, derided at the time, have since been vindicated. His six-volume work on *The Origin and Progress of Language* (1773–92) may seem to the modern reader a rather confused medley of *a priori* guesses, but it made many shrewd points that ran counter to the received views of the day and his account of man's ape-like ancestors anticipated Darwin. His other six-volume work, *Ancient Metaphysics, or The Science of Universals* (1779–99), contains a running attack on modern empiricism which showed a radical misunderstanding of almost all philosophy from Descartes to Hume but at the same time, in vindicating what he considered to be the ancient view of the nature of Mind, Monboddo manages to use both Platonic and Aristotelian notions in developing a theory of evolution that is in some respects startlingly modern. There is a Lamarckian strain in Monboddo's view of the place of Mind in evolution and the ability of the will to affect Nature. His personal oddities—his manner of dress, his Attic banquets where the table was strewn with roses, his excessive addiction to physical exercise, his insistence, when Lord of Session, on sitting not on the bench but at the clerk's table below—made him something of a legend in his own day; but he was an admirable lawyer and a good judge, both learned and upright, not one of whose decisions (often opposed to those of the majority) was ever reversed on appeal to the House of Lords.

James Boswell's father, Alexander Boswell, who took the title of Lord Auchinleck on becoming a Lord of Session in 1754 (he became a Lord of Justiciary in 1755), represented a very different kind of Scottish judge, reminding us that not all the members of the Scottish bench at this time were elegant scholars and men of letters. Auchinleck found Monboddo as antipathetic as he found Dr. Johnson, and it was he who drew attention to Monboddo's eccentric habit of sitting below the bench with the remark, 'Our brother Monboddo, who may say with the psalmist, "De profundis clamavi", is of opinion . . .'[29] Auchinleck can almost be said to have been against the *literati* on principle. He made no attempt to speak fashionable English, but, like his colleague Lord Braxfield, spoke his native Scots on the bench as elsewhere and was indeed one of those Scottish men of law who were responsible for preserving a lively spoken Scots among the legal profession. In commenting on this, Ramsay of Ochtertyre remarked that Auchinleck 'was surely blamable, since the Scots of the seventeenth century had neglected, while it was in their power, to improve their own language. Nothing remained for their descendants', Ramsay went on, 'but to acquire that of their ancient rivals who had brought theirs to a degree of perfection'.[30] This was precisely the view of the majority of the *literati*, and it was this view that Auchinleck, with his belief in common sense, directness, and the validity of the traditional ways of Scotland, strongly disputed. We tend to see Auchinleck today through his son's eyes as an irascible and rather boorish character, but we must remember that he was essentially a patriotic Scottish Whig in the pre-Union tradition whose greatest modern hero was King William and for whom the established Presbyterian Church of Scotland represented the only proper Scottish way to worship. If he was often plain and blunt, he was well educated (like so many Scottish men of law in the eighteenth-century, he studied Roman law in Holland), he had a well-stocked and vigorous mind, and he was a good friend and neighbour on his Ayrshire estate at Auchinleck. He was not generally esteemed a

---

[29] *The Anecdotes and Egotisms of Henry Mackenzie*, edited by H. W. Thompson (London, 1927), p. 111.   [30] op. cit., vol. i, p. 169.

particularly witty man, but Henry Mackenzie records a remark of his which must have been typical of the blunt use he made of his law Latin. An Italian musician named Piscatori was prosecuted for firing a pistol at a man who was attempting to enter his house at midnight in order to visit Piscatori's daughter; the defence pleaded that Piscatori was justified in firing on a *fur nocturnus*. 'I believe', said Lord Auchinleck, 'he was not a *fur nocturnus*; but I believe he was a *furnicator*.'[31]

If Auchinleck is now remembered largely because of his son and of the relations with Dr. Johnson in which his son involved him, Lord Braxfield is generally remembered as the original of Stevenson's Weir of Hermiston. Stevenson's portrait is indeed a reasonable likeness and based on a knowledge of the ascertainable facts, yet there are aspects of the character which were irrelevant to his purpose and are very relevant to ours. Robert MacQueen took the title of Lord Braxfield on becoming a Lord of Session in 1776; he became a Lord of Justiciary in 1780 and Lord Justice-Clerk in 1788. His severity in presiding over the sedition trials of 1793–4 has permanently affected his reputation; yet he was no Judge Jeffries and was indeed a man of high principle with a stern sense of duty and a strong dislike of all the rhetorical frills with which advocates were in the habit of dressing up the plain logic of a legal situation. He was a hard worker, a shrewd and honest lawyer, and a man of uncompromising directness of manner. Like Auchinleck, he made no attempt to modify his native Scots speech on the bench, and sometimes seems to have gone further and deliberately exaggerated it. He enjoyed great popularity as an advocate, and when raised to the bench sacrificed the prospect of making a fortune. His

[31] *Anecdotes and Egotisms*, p. 112.

lack of dignity on the bench and what Ramsay called 'the liveliness, the coarseness, the harshness, of his lordship's expression in trials of life and death',[32] soon destroyed the popularity he had enjoyed as an advocate. But it must be remembered that his coarseness was part of his refusal to come to terms with the genteel Establishment of the *literati*. 'With the *tonish* philosophers and *literati* of Edinburgh', wrote Ramsay, 'he had little connection or correspondence. Certain it is, he disliked their principles, and was aware of their consequences. Nor was he a metaphysician or *belles lettres* scholar.'[33] It would be too much to say that either Auchinleck or Braxfield sensed the instability of the *modus vivendi* between English and Scottish culture achieved by the Edinburgh *literati*, but the attitudes of both these judges expressed kinds of Scottishness which the ideal of the Scottish man of law represented by Lord Kames could not accommodate. It is significant that Kames spoke differently at home and on the bench. 'The language of his social hour', wrote Ramsay, 'was pure Scots, nowise like what he spoke on the bench, which approached to English. In all probability he used the same words, phrases, and articulations which the friends and companions of his younger years made use of in their festive hours, when people's hearts knit to one another.'[34] Here we have precisely that division between the language of the heart and the language of the head that I discussed in my first lecture as one of the consequences of the linguistic position of eighteenth-century Scotland. 'When emotion and thought are separated', Edwin Muir once remarked, with reference to the language of Scottish literature in the eighteenth century, 'emotion becomes irresponsible and

[32] op. cit., vol. i, p. 386.   [33] ibid., pp. 391–2.
[34] ibid., pp. 211–12.

thought arid'.[35] This is only one of the several kinds of cultural schizophrenia found so often in Scotland after the Union, and first found so conspicuously in the poetry and activities of Allan Ramsay. While the law in eighteenth-century Scotland did provide some kind of focus for Scottish culture, and encouraged historians, antiquaries, philosophers and men of letters as well as writers on law, it did not—indeed, it could not—succeed in providing a basis for national culture or for any culture that took into account all the relevant and available traditions of Scottish thought and feeling. We must remember, too, that the law in eighteenth-century Scotland was the road to political office, and that Scottish political life was a wholly *managed* business for a hundred years after the Union—managed, that is, by a nominee of the London government. The higher up a man of law climbed in eighteenth-century Edinburgh, the more he had to keep his eye on the way things were going in London. Those who did not develop cultural schizophrenia were liable to develop a political squint.

I have picked out only a handful of distinguished Scottish men of law in the latter part of the eighteenth century in Scotland; the full story is richer and more fascinating than this. Twenty-seven of the characters depicted in Kay's *Edinburgh Portraits* are judges or advocates or began as men of law, and each is a man of real originality of character, while the valuable biographical index to H. W. Thompson's edition of *The Anecdotes and Egotisms of Henry Mackenzie* contains some seventy Scottish legal characters nearly all of whom are described also as something else (often historian, antiquary or man of letters). Some of the most interesting and the most brilliant I have not mentioned at all. But my purpose

[35] *Scott and Scotland*, by Edwin Muir (London, 1936), p. 29.

is not to write a history of the literary activities of Scottish men of law in the eighteenth century; it is to inquire briefly into the degree to which the law, as one of the two Scottish national institutions surviving after the Union of 1707, was able to provide an adequate focus for a full-blooded Scottish culture. It was hardly to be expected that it could, for however liberally the legal profession is conceived it cannot embrace or include or give expression to the whole of national life. In the circumstances, the law did remarkably well. If it did not solve the problems of post-Union Scottish culture at least it illuminated some of them and it also produced a great variety of interesting minds and talented writers. When Scott in *The Heart of Midlothian* makes Mr. Saddletree hold forth at length about Scots law, in language he misuses and does not adequately understand, in connexion with a tragic situation whose implications he never realizes, or when in *Redgauntlet* he shows how the law in Scotland can both take over from an earlier national tradition of heroic violence and at the same time destroy and corrupt, he is exploring both the opportunities and the limitations of law as a national institution in a modern Scotland. The opportunities were greatest in the late eighteenth and early nineteenth centuries—the age of Lord Kames and the age of Lord Jeffrey—and have declined ever since.

III. The Heavenly City of the Edinburgh Philosophers

On 17 April 1767 the Town Council of Edinburgh formally decided to 'appoint the Dean of Guild and his Council to admitt and receive James Craig architect in Edinburgh to be Burges & Gild-brother of this City agreeable to a minute of the Bridge Committee of the 26th August last bearing him to be entitled to the primum for the best plan of a New Town in terms of the advertisement in the newspapers for that purpose dispencing with the dues for good services'. A few weeks later the Magistrates of Edinburgh formally presented James Craig with a gold medal 'as a reward of his merit for having designed the best plan of the New Town'.[1]

Craig's prize-winning plan represented the culmination of a movement for extending the city of Edinburgh north of what was then the Nor' Loch and what is now Princes Street Gardens. This was more than a town-planning venture designed to relieve the growing congestion in the Old Town which had grown up over the centuries along the ridge between the Castle and Holyrood in a herring-bone pattern with one long street from which led off some sixty closes and wynds.

---

[1] *The Book of the Old Edinburgh Club*, vol. xxiii (Edinburgh, 1940), p. 8. The volume reproduces an early proof of Craig's plan, which was published in January 1768.

It represented, to some at least of the Edinburgh *literati* and to the architect himself, a vision of an ideal city laid out with a rationality, an elegance and a symmetry that mirrored the intellectual ideals of the Enlightenment. Craig was a nephew of the poet James Thomson, who had left his native Scotland to seek his literary fortune in England, and he appended to his plan the following lines from the concluding part of his uncle's poem, 'Liberty':

> August, around, what Public Works I see!
> Lo! stately Streets, lo! Squares that court the breeze!
> See long Canals and deepened Rivers join
> Each part with each, and with the circling Main
> The whole enlivened Isle.

These lines are spoken, in Thomson's poem, by the Goddess of Liberty, who, in the words of the poet's own synopsis, 'points out the chief virtues which are necessary to maintain her establishment there [i.e. in Great Britain.] Recommends, as its last ornament and finishing, Sciences, Fine Arts, and Public Works ... The whole concludes with a Prospect of Future Times, given by the Goddess of Liberty: this described by the Author, as it passes in vision before him'. It is from this final vision that the lines quoted by Craig are taken.

The New Town did not develop exactly as Craig planned, though it followed his general design. Craig intended to preserve the Nor' Loch in the form of a 'long canal' as pictured in his uncle's poem, flanked by tree-planted walks, with the whole valley laid out as a formal park. In general his whole conception was more formal and symmetrical than was finally found practicable or desirable. Nevertheless, the formality and symmetry were not abandoned, and are visible even to the casual eye today. Another point on which some of Craig's original intentions had to be abandoned concerned the naming of the streets. The new street running east and west immediately north of the canal and formal park was to be called—as the existing early proof of the plan shows—Saint Giles Street, after Edinburgh's patron saint. But when the plan was shown to George III, who appears to have had no idea of St. Giles's ancient connexion with the city, he exclaimed, 'Hey, hey!—what, what!—St. Giles Street!—never do, never do!' and the name was altered to Princes Street, after the future George IV and the Duke of York.[2] A similar change from a name with Scottish to one with British associations was indicated by the alteration of Forth Street to Queen Street: George Street, however, was so named from the beginning.

I do not intend to tell the fascinating story of the building of Edinburgh's New Town, which, in spite of subsequent blunders and vulgarizations, remains one of the most beautifully planned urban areas in Europe. I cite Craig's plan because it is so irresistibly symbolic of the idea of civilization cherished by the Edinburgh *literati*. In Carl Becker's brief but classic study of the mind of the Enlightenment, *The Heavenly City of the Eighteenth Century Philosophers*, though he dealt much with Hume and mentioned other Scottish writers and thinkers, he never had occasion to remark that in Edinburgh not only was there a heavenly city implied in the thought of the Scottish moralists of the period—particularly those of the 'moral sense' school—but there was an actual attempt to realize that city in stone. The Goddess of Liberty's speech, from which Craig quoted, was a vision of the future, an optimistic vision of progress. It applied to Great Britain, not simply to England or Scotland. The Scotland of most of the

2 *Old and New Edinburgh*, by James Grant (London, 1882), vol. ii, p. 117.

Edinburgh *literati* was, like Thomson's, 'North Britain', and the changes in the names of St. Giles Street and Forth Street are symbolic of this. Ordered, elegant, rational, optimistic— these are terms which apply equally to Craig's plan and to the dominant thought in the Edinburgh of his time. And most of those who thought in this way were anxious that their thought should go forth to the world in a pure English style, untainted with any Scottish forms, the work of patriotic Scotsmen who had nevertheless sublimated their Scottishness into a comprehensive Britishness.

Looking at Craig's map and reading the words of his uncle that he quotes, we can almost hear so much of what the *literati* were saying in eighteenth-century Edinburgh.

The more of nature is explored and known, the less of evil appears. New discoveries, of wisdom, order and good intention, have always kept pace with increasing learning and knowledge: an intimation, not obscure, of its being owing to our imperfect discoveries and bounded views, that evil is supposed to take place at all.[3]

All mankind so far resemble the good principle, that, where interest or revenge or envy perverts not our disposition, we are always inclined, from our natural philanthropy, to give the preference to the happiness of society, and consequently to virtue above its opposite. Absolute, unprovoked, distinterested malice has never perhaps place in any human breast.[4]

...in natural philosophy, astronomy, chemistry, and other sciences that depend on an extensive knowledge and observation of facts, modern philosophers have an unquestionable superiority over the ancient ... In some studies too, that relate to taste and fine writing ... the progress of society must, in equity, be admitted to have given us some advantages. For instance, in history, there is certainly more political knowledge in several European nations at

---

[3] *Essays on the Principles of Morality and Natural Religion* [by Lord Kames] (Edinburgh, 1751), pp. 388–9.
[4] *An Enquiry concerning the Principles of Morals*, by David Hume, ed. Selby-Bigge (Oxford, 1902), p. 227.

present than there was in ancient Greece and Rome. We are better acquainted with the nature of government . . . The world is more open than it was in former times; commerce is greatly enlarged; more countries are civilised; posts are every where established; intercourse is become more easy; and the knowledge of facts, by consequence, more attainable . . . In the more complex kinds of poetry, likewise, we may have gained somewhat, perhaps, in point of regularity and accuracy.[5]

Finally, to illustrate that the belief in a humane reasonableness, so characteristic of the period, goes side by side not only with a belief in progress but also with a deep belief in the uniformity of human nature and the universal applicability of common sense, I quote this characteristic praise of William Robertson by Dugald Stewart:

The good-sense, temper, and address, with which he presided for thirty years in our University meetings, were attended with effects no less essential to our prosperity; and are attested by a fact which is perhaps without a parallel in the annals of any other literary community; that during the whole of that period, there did not occur a single question which was not terminated by an unanimous decision.[6]

One cannot, of course, present the thought of the Scottish Enlightenment by quoting out of their contexts a few sentences from substantial works: my intention is not so much to present that thought—in any case, hardly a task to be accomplished in a single lecture—as to diagnose what might be called its cultural significance. The elegant symmetry of Craig's plan and the humane optimism about the nature of

[5] *Lectures on Rhetoric and Belles Lettres*, by Hugh Blair (Edinburgh, 1813), vol. iii, p. 10.

[6] *Account of the Life and Writings of William Robertson* [by Dugald Stewart], (London, 1801), p. 197. It is significant that Stewart, in the midst of his lavish praise for Robertson, pauses to point out as a 'defect' that 'his pronunciation and accent were strongly marked with the peculiarities of his country', though his written work was free of 'Scotticisms' (p. 194).

the good city shown in his quotation from Thomson represent an important part of the climate of opinion in which a considerable section of the Scottish *literati* moved. They called Edinburgh the 'Athens of the North' and consciously practised civilization. They were patriotic Scotsmen, making their contribution to the cultural life of Scotland's capital city, yet they thought of their country as 'North Britain' and saw Scotland's vindication as the vying with or even surpassing of England in the production of a common British culture. At the same time many of them took a deep interest not only in Scottish history and antiquities but also—though in a curiously theoretical and academic way—in the ancient Gaelic culture of Scotland. But I shall refer later to the strange paradox of eighteenth-century Scottish men of letters exercising themselves over hypothetical or synthetic or faked-primitive Gaelic poetry while they ignored the genuine Gaelic poetry which was being written by a group of remarkable poets under their very noses.

Though the conscious sense of an urban culture to be found in Edinburgh in the latter half of the eighteenth century was very much a product of its time, it outlived the period of the Enlightenment if not in any continuous way yet to stimulate the imagination of at least one twentieth-century enthusiast for the culture of cities. It is interesting to set the ideas of Sir Patrick Geddes about the organic nature of a city's growth, with his concepts of the relationship between environment, function, and growth and the associated relationship between place, work, and folk beside the ideas implicit in Craig's plan. And Geddes was the teacher of Lewis Mumford, through whom many of his ideas about urban culture and its relation to city planning reached a wider public on both sides of the Atlantic.

The element of conscious planning in the urban and cultural life of late-eighteenth-century Edinburgh was of course intermittent and only partially realized, and it existed side by side with a large number of social and intellectual activities—at the university, in private houses, in the taverns, clubs, and societies in which the city abounded—that cannot be fitted in to any simple scheme or accounted for by any single comprehensive explanation. In the opening chapter of his book on Henry Mackenzie (which is really an account of the literature of late-eighteenth- and early-nineteenth-century Edinburgh), Harold Thompson describes the period, as others had done before him, as the Golden Age of Scotland, and goes on to give an enthusiastic account of its achievement:

> Within Mackenzie's crowded lifetime of eighty-six years [1745–1831] Scotland produced the greatest of sceptical philosophers, David Hume; the best-loved of song-poets, Robert Burns; the king of romancers, Sir Walter Scott; the two chief masters of modern biography, James Boswell and John Gibson Lockhart; the most virile of British portrait-painters, Sir Henry Raeburn; the greatest British architect of his century, Robert Adam. At the same time, the dynasty of the Doctors Monro made Edinburgh's Medical College the most respected in the world; Adam Smith founded the modern science of Political Economy, James Hutton did as much for Geology, and Joseph Black revolutionised Chemistry. Nor was this all; the world's roads were rebuilt according to the methods of John Loudon McAdam; the world's industry was remade by the steam-engine of James Watt; the world's annals of military glory shone with new lustre at the exploits of the most famous of regiments, the Black Watch. Nearly all that makes the name of Scotland great is of that Golden Age; to discover comparable achievements by so small a nation in so short a time we should need to go back from the Age of Mackenzie to the Age of Pericles.[7]

A modern Athens indeed! Yet to run all these names

[7] *A Scottish Man of Feeling*, by Harold W. Thompson (London, 1931), p. 1.

74

together in one triumphant list, however flattering it may be to Scottish pride, is really very misleading. Too many quite different sorts of achievement, stemming from a great variety of factors, are here comprehended, and they do not add up to the manifestation of a national culture. Robert Burns, for example, moving uneasily between an oral folk literature, a partially recovered national 'art' literature, and a genteel English literature, was in a very disturbing relationship with the culture represented by the Edinburgh *literati*, whose advice to him, if he had taken it, would have finished him off as an original poet once and for all. James Boswell, with his love-hate relationship with Scotland and his shame at Scottish speech—to say nothing of his more purely personal obsessions and idiosyncracies—is hardly a product of a national Scottish culture. Scott, with his early imagination nourished by Scottish ballads and German romanticism, cluttered by a passion for Scottish antiquities, and sobered by a study of the law, produced, it is true, a body of literature which reflected exactly this imaginative excitement, this antiquarian clutter and this legal sobriety, and in doing so reflected with equal exactness a moment in Scottish national consciousness. His enchantment with the heroic violence of Scotland's past tempered by a North British sense of where Scotland's future interest lay produced, in his best novels—those that deal with seventeenth- and eighteenth-century Scotland—a kind of implicit dialogue about the pros and cons of the Union, about the simultaneous seductiveness and anachronistic meaninglessness of Jacobitism, that really does throw light on some of the central paradoxes of Scottish national culture at the end of the eighteenth and beginning of the nineteenth centuries. But Henry Mackenzie himself, the Scottish man of feeling, with his mixture of sentimentality and shrewdness, is a far from satisfactory Scottish culture-hero. In spite of his zeal for promoting every kind of Scottish cultural inquiry, exemplified in his helping to found the Royal Society of Edinburgh and, more significantly, by his part in founding the Highland Society of Scotland with its interest both in the economics and in the arts of the Highlands, the whole orientation of Mackenzie's thinking was such as to lead him away from the true realities of the Scottish situation. His influential review of Burns's Kilmarnock volume, while it certainly helped to make the reputation of the poet, singled out for praise precisely those poems in which Burns, imitating the strain of moral and sentimental reflection to be found in the later eighteenth-century English poets, suppressed his original genius to produce sententious and rhetorical effusions of comparatively little merit and possessing no relation at all to what might be called the Scottish centre of the poet's imagination. Mackenzie praises Burns's 'solemn and sublime' strains, 'with that rapt and inspired melancholy in which the Poet lifts his eye "above this visible diurnal sphere"', the Poems intitled *Despondency*, *Winter*, *a Dirge*, and the Invocation to *Ruin*, . . . '[8] He defends Burns against those who accused his poetry of 'breathing a spirit of libertinism and irreligion', but concedes that his Muse 'has been a little unguarded in her ridicule of hypocrisy' and that 'there are exceptionable parts of the volume he has given to the public, which caution would have suppressed, or correction struck out'.[9] This is to miss so blatantly the whole point about Burns's genius that the modern reader can hardly restrain his impatience. Yet it must be remembered that this was the view of Burns shared by the *literati*. Mackenzie, in reacting to Burns in this way, was

[8] *The Lounger, a Periodical Paper*, by the Authors of *The Mirror* (London, 1794), vol. iii, p. 269.   [9] ibid., p. 272.

demonstrating the total lack of equipment of the Edinburgh literary establishment to deal with a whole area of imaginative literature.

This lack of equipment was part of the price paid for becoming the Athens of the north. The heavenly city of the Edinburgh *literati* was built too quickly and in a sense too programmatically to have a truly organic relationship to its own past. In matters of language and the literary imagination—and after all the literary imagination works through language and is dependent on the ability of language to express the whole man—they were cut off from the true sources of strength. The elegant squares of Craig's plan make no allowance for the free play of a disturbing imagination (and all true play of the imagination in art is disturbing), but imply that art, like all other cultural activities, simply confirms, illustrates and decorates our knowledge of human nature to provide agreeable recreation for humane and progressive people. And even if this view is crossed with the Mackenzie brand of sentimentality, as it so often was in the late eighteenth century, a sentimentality that admired the effusion of feeling for its own sake and confused the striking of moral and emotional attitudes with the exploration of moral and psychological situations, it does not yield anything of real literary value or significance. Mackenzie's own novel, *The Man of Feeling*, in spite of some passages that show firm and delicate writing, is now largely a historical curiosity, and his other novels are not even that.

Mackenzie's periodicals, *The Mirror* and *The Lounger*, show very clearly that, as Ramsay in his less assured way was trying to do earlier in the century, Mackenzie sought to improve the literary climate of Scotland by imitating the tone and manner of Addison and Steele. And since Edinburgh was not London, the precise tone of Augustan London could not be captured there, and 'our Scottish Addison' (as Scott called Mackenzie in dedicating *Waverley* to him) was too often tempted to give his readers Addison-and-water. And in any case, Addison lived at the beginning of the century in a different country and the tone appropriate to him when addressing his readers was not necessarily appropriate—even if it had been possible to recapture it—in Edinburgh in 1780. Mackenzie was uneasily aware of this. In the last paper in *The Mirror* he apologized to his readers for the deficiencies of his periodical resulting from the fact that Edinburgh was not London:

In point of subject, as well as of reception, the place where it appeared was unfavourable to the Mirror. Whoever will examine the works of a similar kind that have preceded it, will easily perceive for how many topics they were indebted to local characters and temporary follies, to places of public amusement, and circumstances of reigning fashion. But, with us, besides the danger of personal application, these are hardly various enough for the subject, or important enough for the dignity of writing. There is a sort of classic privilege in the very names of places in London, which does not extend to those of Edinburgh. The Canongate is almost as long as the Strand, but it will not bear the comparison upon paper; and Black-friars-wynd can never vie with Drury-lane, in point of sound, however they may rank in the article of chastity. In the department of humour, these circumstances must necessarily have great weight; and, for papers of humour, the bulk of readers will generally call, because the number is much greater of those who can laugh, than of those who can think. To add to the difficulty, people are too proud to laugh upon easy terms with one, of whose title to make them laugh they are not apprised. A joke in writing is like a joke in conversation; much of its wit depends upon the rank of its author.[10]

The more we ponder these words the more we realize that the

[10] *The Works of Henry Mackenzie, Esq.* (Edinburgh, 1808), vol. v, pp. 86–87.

attitude they reflect provides a very uncertain basis indeed for building up a Scottish literary culture which is at the same time national and original and universal.

It was an older man than Mackenzie, however, who was most responsible for setting the critical tone in Edinburgh in the latter half of the eighteenth century. This was Hugh Blair, who represented the Edinburgh literary establishment when Burns was in the city in the winter of 1786-7. Blair was minister of the High Kirk and also Professor of Rhetoric and Belles Lettres at Edinburgh University, the first holder of that chair, which was founded in 1762 after he had already been teaching rhetoric at the university for two years. It was Blair who introduced Macpherson's *Ossian* to the public, first in his preface to *Fragments of Ancient Poetry, collected in the Highlands of Scotland, and translated from the Gaelic or Erse Language*, 1760, and in 1762 in his *Dissertation concerning the Æra of Ossian* prefaced to *The Poems of Ossian* 'collected and translated by James Macpherson'. Nothing is more characteristic of the genial theorizing which so often passed for history and for criticism among the *literati* than Blair's account of Macpherson's alleged translations. He had no trouble at all in demonstrating how it was that such a barbarous age as that in which it was believed these poems were originally composed could 'produce poems abounding with the disinterested and generous sentiments so conspicuous in the poems of Ossian'. The bards, Blair assures us, 'assumed sentiments that are rarely to be met with in an age of barbarism' because they had 'had their minds opened, and their ideas enlarged, by being initiated in the learning of that celebrated order [of the Druids]'. Each prince tried to emulate the flattering portrait painted by the generous bards. 'This emulation continuing, formed at last the general character of

79

the nation, happily compounded of what is noble in barbarity, and virtuous and generous in a polished people'.[11] Thus the acceptance of the genuineness of Macpherson's *Ossian* was bound up with theories about the nature and function of early poetry and with ideas about the proper balance between the primitive and the polished in the good society which were very much in the air at the time, in England as well as in Scotland, and which were shortly to provide Thomas Warton with the theoretical sub-structure of his *History of English Poetry*.

Lord Kames, in an argument as circular as that of Blair, also proved to his own satisfaction the genuineness of Ossian. No modern writer could have imagined primitive society to be as Ossian depicts it; therefore, it must have really been like that and Macpherson's *Ossian* must be genuine. 'Genuine manners never were represented more to the life by a Tacitus nor a Shakespeare. Such painting is above the reach of pure invention: it must be the work of knowledge and feeling.'[12] The *a priori* anthropology of the eighteenth-century critics is often bound up with their theory of language and especially with their theory of the origin of poetry. 'During the infancy of taste', wrote Lord Kames, 'imagination is suffered to roam, as in sleep, without control. Wonder is the passion of savages and of rustics; to raise which, nothing is necessary but to invent giants and magicians, fairy-land and inchantment.'[13] 'It is chiefly in America', wrote Blair, 'that we have had the opportunity of being made acquainted with men in their savage state. We learn from the particular and concurring

---

[11] *The Poems of Ossian, being a literal translation from the original Gaelic into English; with a Dissertation concerning the Æra in which the Poet lived;* . . . collect-ed and translated by James Macpherson (Edinburgh, 1762), pp. xii–xiii.
[12] *Sketches of the History of Man,* by the Honourable Henry Home of Kames (Edinburgh, 1813), vol. i, p. 361.   [13] ibid., p. 155.

accounts of travellers, that, among all the nations of that vast continent, . . . music and song are, at all their meetings, carried on with an incredible degree of enthusiasm; that the chiefs of the tribe are those who signalize themselves most on such occasions; that it is in songs they celebrate their religious rites; that, by these, they lament their public and private calamities, the death of friends, or the loss of warriors; express their joy on their victories; celebrate the great actions of their nation, and their heroes; excite each other to perform great exploits in war, or to suffer death and torments with unshaken constancy. Here then we see the first beginnings of poetic composition, in those rude effusions, which the enthusiasm of fancy or passion suggested to untaught men, when roused by interesting events, and by their meeting together in public assemblies.'[14] The Hebrew poetry of the Bible, the alleged folk literature of North American Indians and Peruvians, Homer, Norse sagas, Ossian, medieval romance, ballads, even Shakespeare, can be lumped together as illustrations of 'primitive' poetry. The zeal for investigating the origins of poetry in this way produced a spate of books throughout Britain in the eighteenth century.[15] The Scottish *literati* were particularly productive. Adam Smith's *Considerations concerning the first Formation of Languages* (1767) and Lord Monboddo's *Origin and Progress of Language* (1773) are two further Scottish contributions worth mention.

A theory of language based on a theoretical anthropology and a theory of poetry based in turn on this and on both a theoretical and an empirical psychology (with both John

[14] *Lectures on Rhetoric and Belles Lettres*, by Hugh Blair (Edinburgh, 1813), vol. iii, p. 83.

[15] For an account of some of the more important of these, see *The Rise of English Literary History*, by René Wellek (Chapel Hill, 1941), chapter 3: 'Ideas on Literary History'.

Locke and neoplatonism also involved) lie behind much of the rhetorical theory of the eighteenth-century Scottish critics. And the fact that so much of this criticism is rhetorical, that is, concerned with the way in which language works to produce different emotional effects on the reader (or, more often in Kames, the way in which such writers as Shakespeare have registered their awareness of the ways in which human passions operate), is largely the result of the anthropological and psychological bias of the critics. And if, following the lead of Francis Hutcheson, the pioneer of the Scottish Enlightenment, they also held that ethical standards can be explained by the presence of an innate 'moral sense' in man, then rhetorical and psychological criticism becomes also moral criticism, for moral feeling is regarded as a form of sensibility. The critic looks for such qualities as 'tenderness and warmth' in a play or a novel; he admires 'generous and noble sentiments' and 'warm and genuine representations of human nature' while deploring 'cold and artificial performances'.[16] This is all part of the movement which historians of European literature term sentimentality and which was by no means confined to Scotland. But it lodged itself more deeply in Scotland than elsewhere, because of the division between the Scottish head and the Scottish heart that history had already produced. It is true that Hugh Blair's lectures on rhetoric were long used as textbooks of the subject, especially in America, and it is true also that there is much in them of permanent interest. But the apparatus of the Enlightenment employed to purvey a rhetorical analysis of works of literature soon produces yet another paradox of Scottish culture, the co-existence of a coolly rational tone and method with a belief in the moral value of feeling. When the rational tone and method disappeared—

[16] Hugh Blair, op. cit., pp. 328–9.

for reasons which it is beyond the scope of this discussion to pursue—Scottish literature was left with the kailyard as its only refuge. The road from Henry Mackenzie's Man of Feeling to Sir James Barrie's Sentimental Tommy is continuous if not altogether straight. What was largely responsible for making the road a *descensus Averni* was the rapid disappearance of everything we associate with the intellectual achievement of David Hume.

Hume was abused but not understood in his lifetime, and among the many who loved him he lived as 'le bon David' without pressing his philosophical insights. He compromised with the *literati*, and indeed it is difficult to see how he could have done otherwise. His was not the kind of creative mind which could directly help to fertilize a national culture: it could only expose the basis of the thought on which such culture as existed operated, and leave it to another generation—and another nation—to see the creative potentialities of this negative task. It is a pity, nevertheless, that when Burns came to Edinburgh in 1786 Hume had been dead ten years and there was indeed no mind among the *literati* as sharp as the poet's own. Robert Chambers put the matter very well a long time ago: 'A few years before, Burns would perhaps have found an even warmer welcome and a more just appreciation; he would certainly have met, at least, one man intellectually his peer in the Select Society and the Poker Club. But David Hume had, in 1786, been dead half a score of years; Lord Kames was gone; and the majority of their more or less brilliant contemporaries were long past their prime. Adam Smith . . . was too ill to see Burns. William Robertson had only ten years to live; Tytler and Lord Hailes even less. It was, in short, the interregnum between Hume and Scott. Burns himself was the man of the age. It strikes us of this day as almost ludicrous that he should have been patronised by men of the undoubted though secondary capacity of Dugald Stewart, Hugh Blair, and Henry Mackenzie.'[17] Something happened in the age of Scott and Cockburn and Jeffrey to restore the glory and even to raise it to a higher pitch, though this was a short-lived and in a sense a final efflorescence; but that is another story.

Dr. Thomas Blacklock, a leading member of the Edinburgh *literati* and well known as poet, critic, and musician in spite of the handicap of blindness, was an early admirer of Burns. It was his letter to the Reverend Mr. George Lawrie of Kilmarnock which first showed Burns that his reputation had reached the capital. 'There is a pathos and delicacy in his serious poems,' wrote Blacklock; 'a vein of wit and humour in those of a more serious turn, which cannot be too much admired nor too warmly approved.'[18] We can tell something of Blacklock's critical standards from the works of contemporary Scottish criticism I have already discussed. We can learn more, and more directly, from looking at what he wrote himself and what he habitually admired. Blacklock 'and other Scotch gentlemen' published in 1760 a 'collection of original poems' that is unrelieved in its badness.[19] The first, by Blacklock himself, is entitled 'To Two Sisters on their Wedding-day: an Epistle', and opens thus:

> Dear Ladies, whilst the nuptial hour at hand
> Must all your time, and all your thoughts demand,
> Though all the Nine my tuneful strain inspir'd,
> My heart though all the force of friendship fir'd,
> Though warmed with transport for my lovely theme,
> I wou'd not long your kind attention claim;

[17] *The Life and Work of Robert Burns*, edited by Robert Chalmers, revised by William Wallace, Edinburgh, 1896, vol. ii, p. 23.

[18] ibid., vol. i, p. 417.

[19] *A Collection of Original Poems*, by The Rev. Mr. Blacklock, and other Scotch Gentlemen (Edinburgh, 1760).

> Yet let me join the gratulating throng,
> And breathe to Heav'n one ardent wish in song:
> That all your future days, serene and bright,
> May flow distinguished by sincere delight;
> That full success your wishes may attend,
> And Heav'n's best blessings on your heads descend; . . .

Here is the opening of a drinking song by another contributor:

> With roses and with myrtles crown'd,
> I triumph; let the glass go round.
> Jovial Bacchus, ever gay,
> Come, and crown the happy day;
> From my breast drive every care;
> Banish sorrow and despair:
> Let social mirth, and decent joy,
> This delightful hour employ.

This genteel versification, done by the book with such a total lack of any interesting or original use of language that after a while one wants to scream, represents what one might call the establishment poetry of the Edinburgh *literati*—a pale, pale copy of English Augustan verse. This sort of thing can be found in the most unexpected places in eighteenth-century Scottish literature—even in song collections, side by side with sprightly Scots songs in the true folk tradition. The setting of stilted English words to native Scottish airs had been going on since very early in the century—Allan Ramsay had produced some of the most awful—but it still takes one aback to find, for example, in a collection of songs published at Edinburgh in 1765, the following, to the tune of 'The Highland Laddie':

> Now all thy virgin-sweets are mine,
>   And all the shining charms that grace thee;
> My fair Melinda, come recline
>   Upon my breast, while I embrace thee,

> And tell, without dissembling art,
>> My happy raptures on thy bosom:
> Thus will I plant within thy heart,
>> A love that shall for ever blossom.[20]

How salutary, as Matthew Arnold would say, how very salutary after this to turn to Burns on the same theme:

> I hae been blythe wi' comrades dear;
>> I hae been merry drinking;
> I hae been joyfu' gath'rin gear;
>> I hae been happy thinking:
> But a' the pleasures e'er I saw,
>> Tho' three times doubl'd fairly,
> That happy night was worth them a',
>> Amang the rigs o' barley.

When Burns visited Ramsay of Ochtertyre in 1787 Ramsay asked him whether the Edinburgh *literati* 'had mended his poems by their criticisms. "Sir," said he, "these gentlemen remind me of some spinsters in my country, who spin their thread so fine that it is neither fit for weft nor woof". He said he had not changed a word except one, to please Dr. Blair.'[21] Ramsay himself advised Burns to write Scottish Georgics and to write a play based on a Highland tradition about one Omeron Cameron, who sheltered the Earl of Mar in his humble cottage when the earl was in hiding from his enemies. Eventually forced into exile himself, Omeron went to the earl's castle with his wife and children, 'to claim a requital from the earl, who had bidden him do so if ever misfortune should befall him. Upon hearing who it was, the earl started from his seat with a joyful exclamation, and caused Omeron to be conducted with all possible respect into the hall.

[20] *The Charmer: a Choice Collection of Songs, Scots and English* (Edinburgh, 1765), p. 187. The 1765 edition was the third.
[21] *Life and Work of Robert Burns*, ed. Chambers and Wallace, vol. ii, pp. 194–5.

He afterwards conferred on him a four-merk land near the castle'.[22] When one realizes how many admirers and well-wishers, many of them of great reputation or of wealth and influence or of both, were giving Burns this sort of advice, one marvels at his strength of mind and his self-confidence in accepting it so rarely.

He had a hard enough task even without such pressures. He had begun as a local poet, and his most brillaint early poetry reflects his response to local church politics and other aspects of life as lived in his immediate environment. It was produced for his friends who shared his reactions. He soon widened his aim and sought to be a national rather than merely a local Scottish poet. But the materials for a Scottish national poetic tradition were not really to hand. Burns drew on what sources he could, both Scottish and English, and developed a variety of styles and idioms reflecting different uses of these sources. His greatest successes were in satirical poetry, where he drew on a variety of older Scottish traditions but showed also that he had learned certain kinds of verbal discipline from the English Augustans; in counterpointing the familiar and the formal, as for example in his verse letters, a Scottish mode he had learned from Hamilton of Gilbertfield, Allan Ramsay, and Robert Fergusson; in his songs, where at his best he identified himself completely with the folk tradition and saw himself as a national poet using themes and survivals from all over Scotland; and in his single narrative poem, where he invented a beautifully craftsmanlike vehicle for presenting, enriching, and subtilizing material supplied by popular superstition. His language varied from conventional eighteenth-century English parnassian to a Scots in which his native dialect was enlarged by words from other regions and even

[22] ibid.

87

occasionally from older Scottish literature; his most successful idiom was often an English tipped with Scots. Burns's achievement represented a highly precarious balancing between a number of conflicting forces; it was a *personal* achievement, and was not available for fruitful imitation. Even if the industrial revolution had not shortly afterwards so changed the face of a large part of south-west Scotland that later generations used Burns to project their own sentimental nostalgia for a lost and hence idealized rustic way of life, it would still have been unlikely that Burns's synthesis could have been handed on unspoilt. For the social, cultural, and linguistic situation was changing all the time, and Burns's unstable equilibrium soon became an impossibility. This partly explains why it was generally Burns's weakest poems, those in which he posed as a man of feeling and gestured histrionically to an audience prepared to accept him as (in Henry Mackenzie's words) a 'Heaven-taught ploughman', that were most praised in the nineteenth century, why his strength as a satirist was largely ignored and why only a tiny minority of his songs, and those not the best, ever became widely popular. It was not Burns's fault but his misfortune deriving from the historical moment in which he lived, that his weakest side should have been most imitated and, as a result, that he has not proved a good influence on Scottish poetry. The nineteenth century accepted the view of Burns held by the Edinburgh *literati* in Burns's lifetime, ignoring the fact that this view was conditioned partly by an interest in demonstrating the natural moral sensibility of a peasant poet (and thus exaggerating Burns's lack of education) and partly by a rhetorical view of poetry that tended to over-rate a facile appeal to the emotions.

The tensions between Burns and the *literati* were social as well as literary and were made all the more complicated by the poet's genuine feeling of deference towards high formal education and literary reputation and his uncritical admiration of much that was weakly sentimental in eighteenth-century English literature. These existed side by side with his pride, his self-confidence, and his preference for his own modes of writing. The result was psychological pressures and confusions which must have been largely responsible for the erratic and sometimes outrageous behaviour of his last years.[23] That Burns had been accepted by the *literati* was due to his status in their eyes as a natural man, a sort of noble savage. If, like his immediate predecessor in the practice of Scottish poetry, Robert Fergusson, he had come from the city, he would have been ignored by the Edinburgh literary establishment as Fergusson was ignored. Fergusson, who was educated at Dundee High School and St. Andrews University (though he had to leave the latter without completing his course in order to support his widowed mother), had none of the nervous defensiveness about the *literati* occasionally shown by Burns. Nor did he have to pose as an unlettered peasant. He had the confidence to mock Henry Mackenzie's sentimentality with his poem 'The Sow of Feeling' and to parody Dr. Johnson's vocabulary in 'To Dr. Samuel Johnson, food for a new edition of his Dictionary'.

Born in Edinburgh of Aberdeenshire parents and educated in Angus and Fife, Fergusson was able to draw on the Scots vernacular of all these regions when he decided that he wanted

---

[23] Of the truth of this description of Burns's behaviour during his Dumfries period there can be no doubt after the publication of *James Currie The Entire Stranger and Robert Burns*, by R. D. Thornton (Edinburgh, 1963). I take this opportunity of pointing out that in the light of Mr. Thornton's findings and arguments I should want to alter the first paragraph of chapter 7 of my own book, *Robert Burns* (New York, 1951; London, 1952).

to write Scots poetry and revive the Scots poetic tradition. In the few years between his commencing Scots poet and his death in 1774 at the age of twenty-four in the public bedlam of Edinburgh, Fergusson established himself as essentially the poet of Edinburgh, capturing in his racy and craftsmanlike Scots verse the city's rich and varied atmosphere—social, convivial, legal, economic, above all human. He also, in 'The Farmer's Ingle', produced a domestic poem of rustic life which is more perfectly wrought and more consistent in tone than Burns's imitation of it, 'The Cotter's Saturday Night'. True, Fergusson's range was narrow, but that was because he worked with materials that he had lived with: in his Scots poems he showed a concentration and an integrity far greater than Allan Ramsay's and was able to project with colour, vivacity, ironic humour, and brilliance the very essence of Edinburgh life—especially its street life—on the eve of the movement away from the Old Town to the developing New Town. Fergusson's Edinburgh is not the heavenly city of the *literati*. It is still visibly the descendant of Dunbar's Edinburgh, a lusty, dirty, bustling, vivid city pent up on the ridge between the Castle and Arthur's Seat. And Fergusson's convivial evenings at Walter Scott's tavern in Geddes Close with fellow members of the Cape Club or taking his oysters and gin at Lucky Middlemass's or his dish of rizzard haddock and bicker of tippeny at some other Edinburgh howff— these were rather different from the more formal meetings of the Select Society which took place on Friday evenings to discuss literary and philosophical topics and to enable its members to improve themselves in the art of public speaking. It is true that the social lines were not clearly drawn in eighteenth-century Edinburgh when it came to matters of conviviality in taverns, and some very highly placed people could be found enjoying plebeian food and drink in some fairly low places of public resort. Nevertheless, there was a clear difference between the Cape Club on the one hand and the Select Society or the Poker Club on the other. It was not a question of degree of riotousness, for the clubs with the more distinguished members could be very riotous indeed. Judges and advocates were as deep drinkers as poor poets, and the goings-on in 'The Feast of Tabernacles', a club composed of highly placed lawyers and men of letters, proved that it had what Ramsay of Ochtertyre politely called its 'frolicsome moments' as well as the Cape. But the Cape Club was united by a sense of community which drew no social or professional lines at all: in Fergusson's time it included David Herd, the distinguished antiquary and song collector, a number of painters, printers, musicians, and many tradesmen. 'Unlike the aristocratic and therefore socially homogeneous *Poker Club* and *Crochallan Fencibles*', a distinguished student of the subject has written 'the Knighthood of the Cape was a thoroughly democratic institution. The guild of writers sent many members, but tradesmen were in the great majority: shoemakers, tailors, glovemakers, smiths, saddlers, marble-cutters, barbers, brewers were admitted; and that the masters were not void of the necessary humour appears from many a merry document now hidden in the solemn volumes of the club. With them sat a few advocates, writers to the signet, surgeons and doctors, shipowners and naval officers; even a solitary student of divinity appears in the list'.[24]

Fergusson, then, had a sense of the organic life of Edinburgh of a fuller and richer kind than that available to those who saw the city in terms of Craig's plan for the New Town. He

---

[24] *Songs from David Herd's Manuscripts*, edited with Introduction and Notes by Hans Hecht (Edinburgh, 1904), p. 38.

tried to draw on the fading Scots language to find an idiom through which he could capture this sense and in this he was remarkably successful. But both the language he used and the city whose atmosphere he captured in it were passing away. Scots was an unstable and diminishing medium, while the old Edinburgh that Fergusson celebrated was giving way to the New Town in the north as it eventually would also to suburbs in the south leaving the High Street with its wynds and closes to the impoverished and the curious. What Fergusson would have achieved had he lived one can only surmise; he might even have restored temporarily a living Scottish urban poetic tradition. But he could have not restored it permanently, for history was against him.

Ramsay, Fergusson, and Burns, then, represented different moments in the attenuation of the Scottish poetic tradition in the eighteenth century. The confusions and self-contradictions in Ramsay's work and attitude reflect very accurately the cultural predicament of the Scotland of his day. With Fergusson and Burns the trend of history was momentarily deflected by the force of individual genius. Fergusson never came to terms with the literary establishment of the Scotland of his day, and Burns did so only by posing as a Heaven-taught ploughman and at the cost of seeing his best and most characteristic work undervalued. But a realization of these facts must not be allowed to blind us to each poet's remarkable and unpredictable genius. Burns created an Indian summer of the Scottish poetic tradition: his work was not the beginning of a new romanticism but, as Lord Chancellor Seafield had said of Scotland's last act of parliament, 'the end of an auld sang'.

If the Edinburgh *literati* had no use for the Scots vernacular tradition and accepted it only when it was embodied in a poet whom they could regard with interest as confirming their theories about the nature of untutored sensibility (and even then with reservations), what are we to say about their relationship with the Scottish Gaelic tradition? This is a large subject—too large for adequate treatment in a lecture of this kind—but a word must be said about it if the whole picture of eighteenth-century culture is not to appear quite distorted. The *literati* were indeed interested in the Highlands, as is witnessed by their deep concern with Macpherson's *Ossian* and the part that, for example, Henry Mackenzie played in the foundation and activities of the Highland Society. The plight of the Highlands after the Forty-five, the insoluble problems resulting from 'an expanding population within a rigid agrarian economy which offered no hope of a rise in the standard of living',[25] the horrors of the Highland clearances and forced emigration, are part of a sad and complicated story which involves politics and economics more than the cultural questions which we are now considering. But the aftermath of the Forty-five did have cultural consequences: it aroused an interest in the history and literature of Gaelic Scotland and at the same time it ensured that this interest would be distorted by certain romantic preconceptions. This distortion was assisted by the kind of interest in primitive poetry professed by the *literati*. These considerations help to explain why the whole Ossianic controversy which followed the publication of Macpherson's work was largely misdirected: instead of inquiring into the degree to which Macpherson used Gaelic ballads and traditional oral sources in putting together his epics, they searched for ancient manuscripts composed by a bard called Ossian in

[25] *An Economic History of Scotland in the Eighteenth Century*, by Henry Hamilton (Oxford, 1963), p. 101.

93

the third century A.D. It is true that the ultimate result of the controversy was to stimulate inquiry into oral tradition in the Highlands, but the immediate task was misconceived. We now know, thanks to the detailed investigation of Professor Derick Thomson, that Macpherson 'in the course of his writings made use of some fourteen or fifteen Gaelic ballads'[26] and also that 'Macpherson's refining and bowdlerising pen has often changed the atmosphere of the ballads almost beyond recognition'.[27] Macpherson was not translating an ancient epic, and Hume and Blair and Mackenzie, who believed that he was, were wrong. They were wrong partly because they were so out of touch with the realities of Scottish Gaelic literature.

There is something very ironical about the spectacle of the intellectual leaders of Edinburgh theorizing about the nature of Gaelic poetry while ignoring the original Gaelic poetry being written in the Scotland of their own day. There was indeed something of a Gaelic poetic renaissance in eighteenth-century Scotland. This was an indigenous Scottish movement, in which for the first time Scottish Gaelic developed a tradition independent of the formal rhetorical training of the Irish schools; it was a popular movement, too, to such an extent that some of the poets—Rob Donn Mackay and Duncan Ban Macintyre for example—were unable to read or write and had their poems written down for them by others. There is a special irony about Rob Donn's poetry, which seems to have been influenced by Pope, to which indeed it has been compared: it is said that his parish minister, the Rev. Murdoch Macdonald, had not only translated some of Pope into Gaelic but actually made use of these translations in

---

[26] *The Gaelic Sources of Macpherson's 'Ossian'*, by Derick S. Thomson (Edinburgh, 1951), p. 10. [27] ibid., p. 84.

his monthly prayer meetings.[28] So while exploiters of the Celtic twilight were using Macpherson's rhetoricized and sentimentalized adaptations of Gaelic poetry to blow the Pope tradition sky high, an actual practising Gaelic poet was imitating Pope! But this is a minor point. More important is the fact that the first printed work by a Scottish writer written in what could be called Scottish Gaelic as distinct from Irish Gaelic was the small collection of poems published for Alexander Macdonald in Edinburgh in 1751 with the significant title *Ais-eiridh na Sean Chanain Albannaich*, or *Revival of the Old Scottish Tongue*. It is said that, because of the fiercely Jacobite poems it contained, copies were burned by the common hangman in Edinburgh in 1752 by order of the Government.[29] There is a symbolic irony about this, too.

The Jacobite movement had its effect on Gaelic poetry to an even greater extent than it had on Scots song, and we need not pause once again to note the paradox which made the Stuart line in the eighteenth century the champion of Scottish nationalism and the cause of the Highlander. Alexander Macdonald, known among Gaelic speakers as Alasdair MacMhaighstir Alasdair, the greatest of the eighteenth-century Scottish Gaelic poets, was oddly poised between a number of different worlds. Son of an Episcopalian minister in Moidart, Macdonald was partly educated at Glasgow University and turned Presbyterian in order to get a job for a time as catechist in his native part of Scotland. Such positions had been made possible by the earlier formation at Edinburgh of a society for the establishment of charity schools throughout the Highlands and by the granting by George I in 1725 of a sum to be employed similarly, to be administered through the

[28] *The Literature of the Highlands*, by Magnus Maclean (London, n.d.), pp. 94–95.   [29] ibid., p. 42.

General Assembly. Born an Episcopalian, turning to Presbyterianism in order to get a job, Macdonald eventually turned Roman Catholic presumably under the pressure of that Jacobite nationalism which led him to join Prince Charlie's army and to become almost the official bard of Jacobitism. His greatest poems are not, however, his Jacobite incitements to martial valour, but those wonderfully elaborated descriptive pieces in which objects and natural features of a landscape are presented with a special kind of exultation and of *Einfühlung* that is characteristic of the Gaelic genius and so unlike anything written in English or Scots in Scotland at this time—or indeed at any time. 'The Birlinn of Clanranald' and the 'The Sugar Brook' are his masterpieces in this mode, but Macdonald had many styles—patriotic, martial, amorous, satirical, didactic, elegiac—none of which have much to do with the reflections on Gaelic poetry that the Edinburgh *literati* were to engage in during the twenty years following the publication of his pioneer volume.

Of the other Gaelic poets of the period, I mention only Duncan Ban Macintyre, who wrote Jacobite, martial, amatory, satiric, and descriptive poems and whose masterpiece, 'Praise of Ben Dorain' shows this poet's version of that characteristic kind of Gaelic poetry of natural description already mentioned. And to show that Gaelic poetry was not the monopoly of Jacobites and that the religious gloom of extreme forms of Protestant enthusiasm was not confined to Lowlanders, we might cite Dugald Buchanan, whose 'spiritual songs' possess a violent concreteness of imagery that can be positively startling. Like Macdonald, but for a longer period and with more conviction, Buchanan held a post as catechist, at Kinloch Rannoch. He was proficient both in English and Gaelic, and collaborated with the Rev. James Stewart of

96

Killin in seeing through the press the first Gaelic version
of the New Testament to be published. It was while engaged
in this activity in Edinburgh that he arranged for the publication of his own poems there in 1767, at the same time attend-
ing classes at Edinburgh University and meeting many of the
literati including David Hume. The confrontation between
the deeply religious Gael and the Lowland sceptic is interesting: Hume challenged Buchanan to quote anything so
impressive and sublime as Shakespeare's *Tempest* Act IV,
scene i, lines 148–158 (the passage ending with 'We are such
stuff as dreams are made on, . . . ') and Buchanan replied by
quoting from Revelation xx. 11–13 ('And I saw a great
white throne . . . ').[30] One would like to see this story as
symbolic of some aspect of the relation between Gaelic and
Lowland culture in eighteenth-century Scotland, but it
cannot be stretched to provide that larger meaning. The truth
is, that in spite of the medley of emotions aroused by the
Jacobite rebellion of 1745, in spite of well-meant efforts to
investigate and help Highland culture and economy on the
part of some of the *literati*, in spite of inquiries into the
background of Macpherson's *Ossian* conducted by critics and
scholars of Edinburgh and elsewhere, there was little fruitful
inter-relation between Gaelic and non-Gaelic culture in
eighteenth-century Scotland. Each was caught up in its own
dilemmas. Those dilemmas were not easily solved: indeed
many of them still face the Scotland of today, reminding us
that the problems and paradoxes of Scottish culture in the
eighteenth century were not only bound up with the past but
also prefigured the future.

[30] *The Spiritual Songs of Dugald Buchanan*, edited by Rev. Donald Maclean,
(Edinburgh, 1913), p. ix.